Contents

Introduction 4

Number 5

FOCUS ON Number placement and
calculations 5
FOCUS ON Ratio 7
FOCUS ON Fractions, decimals and
percentages 8

Working with whole numbers

SOURCE *Top Gear* ratings 10
SOURCE Mileage readings 14
SOURCE Service schedules 18
SOURCE Antifreeze 22
SOURCE Windscreen wash percentage 26
SOURCE Converting between systems 30

Working with fractions, decimals and percentages

SOURCE Capacities – fuel tanks, engine oil,
coolants and windscreen wash 34
SOURCE Tyre tread depths and pressures 38
SOURCE Car emissions 42
SOURCE Choosing takeaways 46

Measures, shape and space 50

FOCUS ON Reading the date and time 50
FOCUS ON Reading scales and measuring 52
FOCUS ON Converting measures 54
FOCUS ON Measuring areas and volume,
and using scale ratios 56

Calculating time

SOURCE Car number plates 58
SOURCE Time sheets 62

Converting measurements and calculating weights and volume

SOURCE Choosing the correct tyres 66
SOURCE Tyre pressure 70

Shape and volume

SOURCE Storing used oil 74

Perimeter, area and scale drawings

SOURCE Planning a staffroom 1 79
SOURCE Planning a staffroom 2 83

Handling data 87

FOCUS ON Extracting data from tables,
charts and graphs 87
FOCUS ON Presenting data on charts
and graphs 89
FOCUS ON Averages 91

Extracting data from tables, charts and graphs

SOURCE Working days lost through
sickness 92
SOURCE Carbon emissions targets 96
SOURCE Accidents on roads 100
SOURCE Power and torque 104

Presenting data on charts and graphs

SOURCE Green cars 108
SOURCE Drink-driving 112

Interpreting data from charts and graphs

SOURCE Car sales 116
SOURCE Petrol costs 120
SOURCE Car servicing 124

Acknowledgements 128

Introduction

> 'National Numeracy is a new charity focussed on transforming public attitudes to maths and numeracy and to seeing a measurable transformation of maths in school and for adults.
>
> We endorse Nelson Thornes' commitment to presenting mathematics in a range of adult-based contexts – school textbooks do not do this well. We also like the fact that they have used data from a range of sources and presented data in a variety of forms found in real-life examples.
>
> To this end, these could be useful resources for encouraging renewed interest from adults in mathematics – mathematics that will appear more appropriate to their daily lives.'
>
> Mike Ellicock
Chief Executive, National Numeracy
www.nationalnumeracy.org.uk

'Functional skills are the fundamental, applied skills in English, mathematics, and information and communication technology (ICT) which help people to gain the most from life, learning and work.'

Ofqual (2012), Criteria for Functional Skills Qualifications

This workbook is designed to present functional maths in a variety of contexts to make it accessible and relevant to you, as Motor Vehicle Technology candidates. It is intended to be written in, so use the extra white space for your workings out!

Being 'functional' means that you will:

- be able to apply skills to all sorts of real-life contexts
- have the mental ability to take on challenges in a range of new settings
- be able to work independently
- realise that tasks often need persistence, thought and reflection.

Features of this workbook are:

 ## FOCUS ON

Each Focus on is typically 1–2 pages long and will teach you specific Functional Skills. They include:

- guidance on the skill
- relevant working examples.

These pages will cover important aspects of Motor Vehicle Technology and consist of interesting source materials, such as newspaper articles or industry-related information, followed by various questions and activities for you to complete.

Good luck!

In Context

Functional Skills Maths

ENTRY 3 –
LEVEL 2

Motor Vehicle Technology Workbook

Deborah Holder
Veronica Thomas

Nelson Thornes

This edition published in 2013 by:
Nelson Thornes Ltd
Delta Place
27 Bath Road
CHELTENHAM
GL53 7TH
United Kingdom

13 14 15 16 17 / 10 9 8 7 6 5 4 3 2 1

A catalogue record for this book is available from the British Library

ISBN 978 1 4085 1835 9

Cover image: Kudryashka/Shutterstock

Artwork: Paul McCaffrey and James Elston at Sylvie Poggio Artists Agency

Page make-up by Pantek Media, Maidstone

Printed in China

Number

Working with whole numbers

Reading and writing numbers

It is important to recognise the value of digits in different columns so that you know the size of the number and can check that your answers are sensible.

	Millions			Thousands					
	H	T	U	H	T	U	H	T	U
Four thousand and sixty-five						4	0	6	5
Forty thousand and sixty-five					4	0	0	6	5
Four hundred thousand, six hundred and fifty				4	0	0	6	5	0
Four million, six hundred and fifty thousand			4	6	5	0	0	0	0
Forty million		4	0	0	0	0	0	0	0

HTU stands for hundreds, tens and units.

Rounding numbers

Rounded numbers can be used for estimation and checking. Numbers can be rounded to the nearest 10, 100, 1000, 10 000, etc. depending on the size of the number and the level of accuracy needed.

- To round to the nearest 100, for example, first find the digit in the hundreds column.

- If the 'deciding digit' in the column to the right is below 5, the digit in the hundreds column stays the same, i.e. the number is rounded down.

- If the 'deciding digit' in the column to the right is 5 or above, the digit in the hundreds column increases by 1, i.e. the number is rounded up.

> **Remember:** if rounding to the nearest <u>10</u>, the number will end in <u>0</u>; to the nearest <u>100</u>, the number will end in <u>00</u>; to the nearest <u>1000</u> the number will end in <u>000</u> etc.

Examples:

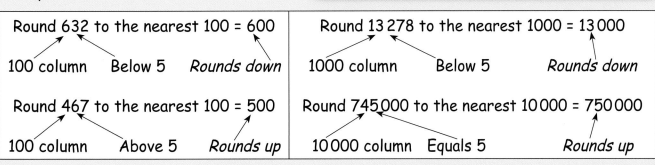

Calculating with whole numbers

Consider the problem and write it down in your own words if this helps.

Decide which numbers you need and whether you need to add, subtract, multiply, divide or carry out more than one of these operations in a particular order.

Check your answer is sensible based on your own knowledge and experience. You can also check it using the techniques shown below.

Checking calculations

Use estimation or the reverse operation to check your calculations.

Examples:

A garage buys a car for £8320 and sells it for £10499. How much money does the garage make on the sale of the car? 10499 – 8320 = 2179 Estimation check: 10500 – 8300 = 2200, so the correct answer is the right size. Reverse calculation check: 2179 + 8320 = 10499	A mechanic is paid £29820 a year. How much is this a month? £29820 ÷ 12 = £2485 Estimation check: 30000 ÷ 10 = 3000, so the correct answer is the right size. Reverse calculation check: £2485 × 12 = £29820

Using formulae

When working with formulae, remember the order of operations can be represented by **BIDMAS**: **B**rackets, then **I**ndices, **D**ivision and **M**ultiplication, **A**ddition and **S**ubtraction.

Examples:

Formula for calculating the area of a circle

$A = \pi r^2$

where A = area and r = radius.

If $\pi = 3.14$ and $r = 5\,cm$

$5 \times 5 = 25$ $25 \times 3.14 = 78.5$ Area = $78.5\,cm^2$

^{2} means multiply by itself

Formula for calculating current

$$I = \frac{V}{(R_1 + R_2)}$$

where I = current (in amps), V = voltage (in volts), and R_1 and R_2 are resistance values (in ohms).

If $V = 12$, $R_1 = 2$ and $R_2 = 4$

$R_1 + R_2 = 6$ $12 \div 6 = 2$ Divide as <u>below</u> the line

FOCUS ON Ratio

Writing ratios

Ratios can be expressed in different ways.

Examples:

'1 in 4 of the staff were unqualified' can be written as:

The ratio of unqualified to qualified staff was 1:3.

'Use 1 part screen wash to 5 parts water' can be written as:

The ratio of screen wash to water should be 1:5.

Simplifying ratios

Simplify ratios by dividing both numbers by a common factor.

Examples:

5:10 can be simplified as 1:2 (divide each side by 5).

120:180 can be simplified as 2:3 (divide each side by 60).

Simplified ratios can then be used to calculate other quantities.

Calculating quantities using ratios

You can use a simple diagram to check that the numbers increase (or decrease) in proportion both horizontally and vertically.

Example:

If the ratio of screen wash to water should be 1:5, how much water should be mixed with 300 ml of screen wash?

Screen wash : Water
$$
\begin{array}{c}
1:5 \quad \Big| \times 300 \\
300:1500 \downarrow \\
\overrightarrow{} \\
\times 5
\end{array}
$$

$300 \times 5 = 1500$ ml

You can also draw a picture to help you visualise the problem.

Example:

1500 ml of diluted anti-freeze and coolant is needed in a ratio of 2 parts anti-freeze and coolant to 3 parts water. How much anti-freeze and coolant and how much water is needed?

Divide the total amount by the total number of parts to find the value of 1 part. Use this to calculate quantities for 2 and 3 parts.

Check: 600 + 900 = 1500 ml

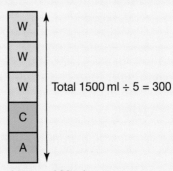

Total 1500 ml ÷ 5 = 300

1 part = 300 ml
2 parts anti-freeze and coolant = 600 ml
3 parts water = 900 ml

Working with fractions, decimals and percentages

 FOCUS ON Fractions, decimals and percentages

Fractions

Fractions look like this and are made up of two different components.

$\frac{1}{5}$ numerator (number of pieces)
denominator (number of equal pieces the whole has been split into)

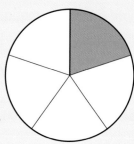

Adding and subtracting fractions

To add or subtract fractions, make the denominators the same. You may need to find an equivalent fraction. For example:

$\frac{1}{2} + \frac{2}{6}$

$\frac{1}{2} \frac{(\times 3)}{(\times 3)} = \frac{3}{6}$ multiplying the top and bottom numbers by the same value

so $\frac{3}{6} + \frac{2}{6} = \frac{5}{6}$

Or you can multiply the denominators together to make them the same.

For example: For $\frac{1}{2} + \frac{2}{6}$, $2 \times 6 = 12$

Then cross-multiply the top and bottom numbers to make equal fractions:

so $\frac{1}{2} + \frac{2}{6} = \frac{(1 \times 6) + (2 \times 2)}{12}$

$= \frac{10}{12}$

Then cancel to the lowest term.

$\frac{10}{12} = \frac{5}{6}$ ($\div 2$)

Multiplying fractions

Multiply the numerators to give the new numerator. Multiply the denominators to give the new denominator. For example:

$\frac{1}{2} \times \frac{1}{4} = \frac{1}{8}$

In words, the above example could be thought of as half of a quarter.

Dividing fractions

Turn one fraction upside-down and then multiply the numerators and denominators as above. For example:

$\frac{1}{2} \div \frac{1}{4} = \frac{1}{2} \times \frac{4}{1} = \frac{4}{2} = 2$

The answer will always be larger.

Percentages

'Percent' means a specific proportion of every 100. For example:

   1% = 1p in every £   or   £1 in every £100

   10% = 10 in every 100 = $\frac{10}{100} = \frac{1}{10}$

> **Remember:** there are 100 pennies in every pound.

To find $\frac{1}{10}$ of a number divide it by 10. Move the numbers one column to the right around the decimal point. For example: 10% of 45 m = 4.5 m

With percentages, always remember to calculate from the starting point. For example, if a shop reduces a £10 grease gun by 10% and then later decides to increase the price by 10%, the price will not return to £10.

Start with £10. 10% of £10 is £1, so the reduced price is £10 - £1 = £9.
Start with £9. 10% of £9 is 90p, so the increased price is £9 + 90p = £9.90.

Decimals

Remember the place values in decimals. This is how decimals are set out:

hundreds	tens	units	decimal point	tenths	hundredths	thousandths
		0	.	2		

2 tenths of whatever the unit is

From example: 0.2 m = $\frac{2}{10}$ of a metre = 20 cm

Always write a zero before the decimal point.
This avoids any confusion with the decimal point.

Remember: there are 100 centimetres in every metre.

Zeros after the final number following a decimal point are not needed. For example: 0.2 = 0.20 = 0.200. However, remember that you always need two decimal places for money.

Adding and subtracting decimals

All the numbers must be in the same units, for example, all centimetres or all metres. Convert them if not. Set out the sum so that all the decimal points align vertically and then add or subtract the numbers in columns.

Multiplying decimals

Ignore the decimal point to start with. Multiply the numbers normally. When you have the numbers in the answer, count the total number of digits after all the decimal points in the sum. Insert the decimal point so that the same number of digits are to the right of it in the answer. For example:

$$\begin{array}{r} 3.14 \\ \times\ 1.6 \\ \hline 5.024 \end{array}$$ 3 digits to the right of all the points

3 digits to the right of the point

Dividing decimals

Multiply both numbers by 10, 100, etc. to remove the decimal point from the dividing number. Then divide as normal. For example:

$3.5\overline{)70.7}$ $35\overline{)707.0} = 20.2$

$\times 10$

Recurring decimals

If a fraction does not divide exactly to make an equivalent decimal value, but has a recurring number or numbers, it is called a recurring decimal. A dot is written above the recurring numbers. For example $\frac{1}{3}$ = 0.333... = 0.3

Working with whole numbers

SOURCE *Top Gear* ratings

As a technician, Jerome has his own views about what makes a car special. He likes to compare his opinions with those of the *Top Gear* team. He is always keen to see the ratings they have given to cars at the cheapest and most expensive ends of the market.

Cars starting from less than £14000		
Make and model	***Top Gear* rating**	**Starting price (£)**
Alfa Romeo MiTo	8/10	11534
Citroen C3 Picasso	8/10	11575
Ford Fiesta	8/10	9415
Fiat Abarth	8/10	9396
Hyundai i10	7/10	7261
Mazda 2	7/10	7824
Mini Clubman	7/10	13720
Nissan Micra	7/10	7820
Renault Clio	7/10	8035
Seat Leon	7/10	13810
Skoda Fabia	7/10	9200
Toyota Aygo	7/10	7745
Vauxhall Corsa	8/10	8240
VW Golf	8/10	12899

Cars starting from more than £50000		
Make and model	***Top Gear* rating**	**Starting price (£)**
Aston Martin DBS	8/10	175891
Bentley Mulsanne	8/10	224700
Bugatti Veyron	9/10	1139000
Ferrari 599	10/10	201500
Jaguar XK	8/10	58380
Lamborghini Aventador	9/10	242280
Maserati Gran Turismo	8/10	77755
Mercedes-Benz CL Class	8/10	90885
Morgan Aero	8/10	66553
Porsche 911	9/10	63023
Rolls-Royce Phantom	9/10	276595

E3

Study the table of cars starting from less than £14 000.

1 Complete the first and second columns of the table below by putting the cars in order of price, starting with the cheapest.

Make and model	Starting price	Rounded to nearest £100

2 a) Write the price of the cheapest car in the table in words.

   b) Write the price of the most expensive car in the table in words.

3 What is the difference in starting price between the

   a) Mazda 2 and Toyota Aygo?

   b) Skoda Fabia and Vauxhall Corsa?

   c) Seat Leon and VW Golf?

4 Complete the third column of the table by rounding the starting prices to the nearest £100.

5 Use the rounded figures to check that your answers to question 3 are the right size.

L1

Study the table of cars starting from more than £50 000.

1   Complete the first and second columns of the table below by putting the cars in order of price, starting with the cheapest.

Make and model	Starting price	Rounded to nearest £10 000

2   Write the starting prices of these cars in words.

a) Porsche 911

b) Aston Martin DBS

c) Rolls-Royce Phantom

d) Bugatti Veyron

3   What is the difference in starting price between the:

a) Mercedes-Benz CL Class and Jaguar XK?

b) Lamborghini Aventador and Ferrari 599?

c) Bugatti Veyron and Rolls-Royce Phantom?

4   Complete the third column of the table by rounding the starting prices to the nearest £10 000.

5   Use the rounded figures to check that your answers to question 3 are the right size.

L2

1 Decide whether the following statements are true or false (use actual prices, not rounded).

a) The starting price of a Mercedes-Benz CL Class is just under £0.1 million.   True ☐   False ☐

b) The starting price of a Ferrari 599 is just over £0.2 million.   True ☐   False ☐

c) The starting price of a Rolls-Royce Phantom is over a quarter of a million pounds.   True ☐   False ☐

d) The starting price of a Bugatti Veyron is just under 1.4 million.   True ☐   False ☐

e) The starting prices of the Jaguar XK, Maserati Gran Turismo, Morgan Aero and Porsche 911 total less than the starting price of the Rolls-Royce Phantom.   True ☐   False ☐

f) The starting price of the Maserati Gran Turismo is more than 100 times the price of the Toyota Aygo.   True ☐   False ☐

g) The starting price of the Lamborghini Aventador is more than 30 times the price of the Renault Clio.   True ☐   False ☐

h) The starting price of the Bugatti Veyron is more than 150 times the price of the Hyundai i10.   True ☐   False ☐

i) You could buy more than 100 Bugatti Veyrons for £1 billion.   True ☐   False ☐

2 Calculate the difference in starting price of the following (use actual prices, not rounded). Give your answer rounded to the nearest £1000.

a) Ferrari 599 and Porsche 911

☐

b) Bentley Mulsanne and Skoda Fabia

☐

c) Bugatti Veyron and Maserati Gran Turismo

☐

d) Bugatti Veyron and Jaguar XK

☐

e) Bugatti Veyron and Hyundai i10

☐

Working with whole numbers

 Mileage readings

Jane works at a garage that buys and sells used cars. She works on the cars before they are sold. She writes down the exact mileage of each car as a colleague reads it out. Jane also finds it useful to use approximate mileage figures when considering what might need repairing or replacing.

Newer used cars

Registration	Mileage
WN62TVW	Seven thousand, two hundred and eighty
VB62OAN	Five thousand, seven hundred and forty-eight
VL12SPC	Ten thousand, three hundred and twenty-one
WA62XRP	Eight thousand, four hundred and forty-five
GB12VWM	Nine thousand, eight hundred and sixty-two
WU12LJC	Nine thousand, eight hundred and six
WP12KTV	Eight thousand, nine hundred and ninety-five
GK62BZE	Six thousand and ninety-four
VR62WAV	Six thousand, two hundred and seventeen
WD12UPD	Ten thousand and seventy-eight
RD12NLR	Nine thousand, two hundred and fifty-five
FM62MKE	Six thousand, seven hundred and twenty-three
WP62LTB	Six thousand, five hundred and seventy-two
GT12MNV	Eight thousand, nine hundred and one

Older used cars

Registration	Mileage
WD58STE	Sixty-seven thousand, eight hundred and five
WG57FLN	Seventy thousand, nine hundred and twelve
RE53VKP	One hundred and eight thousand, five hundred and thirty-six
OVO3JRZ	Two hundred and fifty-four thousand, five hundred and ninety-seven
LS07DBT	One hundred and seventeen thousand, three hundred and forty-eight
RX05NME	Three hundred and fifty-four thousand, six hundred and twenty-one
ONO7SET	Two hundred and four thousand and thirteen
WHO9LKO	One hundred and twenty-five thousand, four hundred and ninety-three
WB07RSC	One hundred thousand, eight hundred and twenty-one

E3

Study the records for the newer used cars.

1 Write the mileage in figures in the second column of the table below.

Registration	Mileage	Rounded to nearest 100 miles
WN62TVW		
VB62OAN		
VL12SPC		
WA62XRP		
GB12VWM		
WU12LJC		
WP12KTV		
GK62BZE		
VR62WAV		
WD12UPD		
RD12NLR		
FM62MKE		
WP62LTB		
GT12MNV		

2 Which car has:

a) the highest mileage?

b) the lowest mileage?

3 What is the difference in mileage between:

a) GB12VWM and WU12LJC?

b) WP12KTV and GK62BZE?

c) WP62LTB and GT12MNV?

d) WD12UPD and RD12NLR?

4 Complete the third column of the table by rounding each mileage figure to the nearest 100 miles. Use the rounded figures to check your answers to question 3.

L1

Study the records for the older used cars.

1 Write the mileage in figures in the second column of the table below.

Registration	Mileage	Rounded to nearest 1000 miles	Rounded to nearest 10 000 miles
WD58STE			
WG57FLN			
RE53VKP			
OV03JRZ			
LS07DBT			
RX05NME			
ON07SET			
WH09LKO			
WB07RSC			

2 Which car has:

a) the highest mileage?

b) the lowest mileage?

3 What is the difference in mileage between the following cars? Give your answers in words.

a) WD58STE and WG57FLN

b) OV03JRZ and LS07DBT

c) ON07SET and WH09LKO

d) RX05NME and ON07SET

4 Complete the third column of the table by rounding each mileage figure to the nearest 1000 miles. Use the rounded figures to check your answers to question 3.

5 a) Complete the fourth column of the table by rounding each mileage figure to the nearest 10 000 miles. (Use the original figures.)

   b) Use these rounded figures to decide which cars fit the following description: 'Less than one hundred and fifty thousand miles on the clock'.

L2

1   Which car's mileage is:

a) just over a quarter of a million miles?

b) over 0.3 million miles?

2   WG57FLN has had one owner who bought it new and drove it for four years. On average how many miles a month did the owner drive? Give your answer to the nearest whole mile.

3   WH09LKO has had one owner who bought it new and drove it for $3\frac{1}{2}$ years. On average how many miles a year did the owner drive? Give your answer to the nearest whole mile.

4   The last owner of ON07SET bought the car with 178 357 miles on the clock. They drove the car for $1\frac{1}{2}$ years. How many miles did they drive on average per month? Give your answer to the nearest whole mile.

5   The last owner of RX05NME bought the car with 225 360 miles on the clock. They drove the car for $4\frac{1}{2}$ years. How many miles did they drive on average per week? Give your answer to the nearest whole mile.

6   WA62XRP was a company car and was used five days a week for six months. On average how many miles a day was the car driven? Give your answer to the nearest mile.

7   WN62TVW was a company car and was used five days a week for three months. On average how many miles a day was the car driven, to the nearest mile?

8   WP12KTV was a company car and was used five days a week for nine months. On average how many miles a day was the car driven, to the nearest mile?

Working with whole numbers

 **Service schedules**

Philippa works at a Honda garage. She refers to the schedule below when servicing cars and advising customers.

2012 Honda Civic Sedan DX 4dr Man

SERVICE SCHEDULE

Service A – After first 3750 miles, then every 3750 miles
Replace engine oil and filter
Inspect fluid levels
Replace drain and plug washer
Inspect tyre pressures
Inspect lights
Inspect horn
Inspect wipers

Service B – After first 7500 miles, then every 7500 miles
Inspect hoses
Inspect front and rear brakes
Inspect exhaust system
Rotate and balance wheels
Inspect drive shaft boots
System road test

Service C – After first 15 000 miles, then every 15 000 miles
Steering alignment
Charging system and belts

Service D – After first 30 000 miles, then every 30 000 miles
Replace air filter
Replace transmission fluid
Replace brake fluid
Replace fuel filter
Clean engine

E3

1 Complete the table to show the recommended mileage for each Service A.

Service	1st	2nd	3rd	4th	5th	6th	7th	8th	9th
Mileage	3750								

Study Service A and answer the following questions.

2 Mr Day's car has 2985 miles on the clock. How many more miles until the first service is due?

3 Mrs Patel's car has 3052 miles on the clock. How many more miles until the first service is due?

4 Mr Wieckowski's car has 4372 miles on clock. He has not had it serviced yet. How many miles overdue is the service?

5 Ms Peter's car has 6732 miles on the clock. How many more miles until the next service is due?

6 Miss Tanner's car has had one service at 3750 miles. There are now 7830 miles on the clock. How many miles overdue is the second service?

7 Mr Fisher buys a car with 4789 miles on the clock. It has just had a service. He wants to follow the schedule and have it serviced again when he has driven 3750 miles. What will the mileage be then?

8 Mrs Lesser drives 125 miles a week. How many weeks will it take her to drive 3750 miles?

9 Mr Singh drives 150 miles a week. How many weeks will it take him to drive 3750 miles?

10 It takes Miss O'Connor 50 weeks to drive 3750 miles. How many miles does she drive on average per week?

L1

1   Mr Carter buys a car with 78 953 miles on the clock. It has just had Services A, B, C and D. If he wants future services to take place after the number of miles given in the schedule, what will the mileages be when the following are due?

a) Service A

b) Service B

c) Service C

d) Service D

2   Mrs Saunders was scheduled to have Services A, B and C when the mileage reached 127 450. However, she drove an extra 5275 miles before getting the car serviced. If she wants future services to take place after the number of miles given in the schedule, what will the mileages be when the following are due?

a) Service A

b) Service B

c) Service C

3   Ms McDonald estimates that she drives 600 miles a month. How many months, according to the schedule, would it be between services for:

a) Service A?

b) Service B?

c) Service C?

d) Service D?

4   Mr Dembenski estimates that he drives 19 500 miles in a year and that this mileage is spread fairly evenly over the year. How many weeks, according to the schedule, would it be between services for:

a) Service A?

b) Service B?

c) Service C?

d) Service D?

L2

1   The following cars have all been serviced according to the schedule. How many miles until each one is due the following services?

a) Car A: mileage 13 826

i) Service A

ii) Service B

iii) Service C

iv) Service D

b) Car B: mileage 27 426

i) Service A

ii) Service B

iii) Service C

iv) Service D

c) Car C: mileage 34 676

i) Service A

ii) Service B

iii) Service C

iv) Service D

d) Car D: mileage 66 542

i) Service A

ii) Service B

iii) Service C

iv) Service D

2   The following cars had their last services (A, B, C and D) at the mileages shown. According to the schedule, how many miles until the next service is due or how many miles is the service overdue?

a) Car A: last full service at 22 357; current mileage 35 765

i) Service A

ii) Service B

iii) Service C

iv) Service D

b) Car B: last full service at 68 540; current mileage 89 253

i) Service A

ii) Service B

iii) Service C

iv) Service D

Working with whole numbers

 Antifreeze

As a technician, Ben needs to be able to follow manufacturers' instructions for diluting antifreeze when servicing different cars. He also needs to consider different driving conditions. Here are the labels from some of the products he has to deal with.

Advanced Antifreeze

Temperatures

| From −18 °C to 108 °C (1 part Antifreeze to 2 parts water) | From −34 °C to −19 °C (1 part Antifreeze to 1 part water) |

Standard Antifreeze

Min (°C)	Max (°C)	Ratio
		Antifreeze : Water
−24	126	2 : 3
−37	129	1 : 1
−52	132	3 : 2
−64	136	5 : 3

(Temperature)

E3

Study the top label, for Advanced Antifreeze.

The instructions say that at temperatures from –34°C to –19°C, equal amounts of Antifreeze and water should be used. For example, 200 ml of Antifreeze should be mixed with 200 ml of water.

1 If the correct amount of water were mixed with each amount of Antifreeze below, what would the total amount of mixture be? Give your answers in ml.

   a) 650 ml of Antifreeze

   b) 800 ml of Antifreeze

   c) 1000 ml of Antifreeze

   d) 1200 ml of Antifreeze

2 To make the total amount of mixture shown below, how much Antifreeze should you use?

   a) 1000 ml of mixture

   b) 1100 ml of mixture

   c) 1750 ml of mixture

   d) 2500 ml of mixture

The instructions say that at temperatures from –18°C to 108°C, twice as much water as Antifreeze should be used. For example, if 100 ml of Antifreeze is used, 200 ml of water should be used.

3 How many ml of water should be mixed with the amounts of Antifreeze shown below?

   a) 200 ml of Antifreeze

   b) 500 ml of Antifreeze

   c) 750 ml of Antifreeze

   d) 900 ml of Antifreeze

4 At temperatures from –18°C to 108°C, how many ml of Antifreeze should be mixed with the amounts of water shown below?

   a) 600 ml of water

   b) 1200 ml of water

   c) 1400 ml of water

   d) 2000 ml of water

L1

Study the bottom label, for Standard Antifreeze.

1 What ratio of Antifreeze to water should you use if driving in the following conditions?

a) Britain: Temperature –10 °C

b) Canada: Temperature –50 °C

c) Croatia: Temperature –18 °C

d) China: Temperature –30 °C

e) Russia: Temperature –58 °C

f) Norway: Temperature –35 °C

2 Which temperature range is each of the following mixtures suitable for?

a) 200 ml Antifreeze : 300 ml water

d) 750 ml Antifreeze : 500 ml water

b) 600 ml Antifreeze : 400 ml water

e) 750 ml Antifreeze : 450 ml water

c) 1500 ml Antifreeze : 1500 ml water

f) 900 ml Antifreeze : 1350 ml water

3 Using the ratio for temperatures from –24 °C to 126 °C, calculate how many ml of water should be mixed with:

a) 200 ml of Antifreeze

c) 500 ml of Antifreeze

b) 400 ml of Antifreeze

d) 1200 ml of Antifreeze

4 Use your answers to question 3 to calculate the total amount of mixture in each case. Give your answers in ml.

a)

c)

b)

d)

L2

Study the bottom label, for Standard Antifreeze.

1 Using the ratio for temperatures from −52 °C to 132 °C, calculate how much water should be mixed with:

a) 750 ml of Antifreeze

b) 540 ml of Antifreeze

c) 1050 ml of Antifreeze

d) 2100 ml of Antifreeze

2 Using the ratio for temperatures from −64 °C to 136 °C, calculate how much water should be mixed with:

a) 250 ml of Antifreeze

b) 750 ml of Antifreeze

c) 1000 ml of Antifreeze

d) 1400 ml of Antifreeze

3 Using the ratio for temperatures from −24 °C to 126 °C, calculate how many ml of Antifreeze and water should be mixed together to make:

a) 1500 ml

b) 2400 ml

c) 3750 ml

d) 4200 ml

4 Using the ratio for temperatures from −52 °C to 132 °C, calculate how many ml of Antifreeze and water should be mixed together to make:

a) 2000 ml

b) 3000 ml

c) 3600 ml

d) 4200 ml

5 Using the ratio for temperatures from −64 °C to 136 °C, calculate how many ml of Antifreeze and water should be mixed together to make:

a) 2400 ml

c) 3600 ml

b) 3000 ml

d) 4200 ml

Working with whole numbers

 **Windscreen wash percentage**

Craig runs a garage and needs to calculate the amount of windscreen wash used so that he can decide which product offers the best value. Here are the labels from two different products.

Regular Windscreen Wash

Windscreen wash : Water

Summer	1:5
Normal use	1:2.5
Winter	1:1

Double Concentrate Windscreen Wash

Windscreen wash : Water

Summer	1:10
Normal use	1:5
Winter	1:1

E3

Study the left-hand label for the regular windscreen wash.

For summer use you need 5 times as much water as windscreen wash. For example, if you use 100 ml of windscreen wash, you need 500 ml of water.

1   How much water would you use with the following amounts of regular windscreen wash?

   a) 50 ml [　　　　　　　]

   b) 200 ml [　　　　　　　]

   c) 300 ml [　　　　　　　]

   d) 500 ml [　　　　　　　]

2   Add your answers from question 1 to the amount of regular windscreen wash to find the total amount of the mixture in each case.

   a) 50 ml windscreen wash + [　　　　] ml water = [　　　　] ml mixture

   b) 200 ml windscreen wash + [　　　　] ml water = [　　　　] ml mixture

   c) 300 ml windscreen wash + [　　　　] ml water = [　　　　] ml mixture

   d) 500 ml windscreen wash + [　　　　] ml water = [　　　　] ml mixture

Study the right-hand label for the concentrated windscreen wash.

For summer use you need 10 times as much water as windscreen wash. For example, if you use 100 ml of windscreen wash, you need 1000 ml of water.

3   How much water would you use with the following amounts of concentrated windscreen wash?

   a) 50 ml [　　　　　　　]

   b) 200 ml [　　　　　　　]

   c) 300 ml [　　　　　　　]

   d) 500 ml [　　　　　　　]

4   Add your answers to question 3 to the amount of concentrated windscreen wash to find the total amount of the mixture in each case.

   a) 50 ml windscreen wash + [　　　　] ml water = [　　　　] ml mixture

   b) 200 ml windscreen wash + [　　　　] ml water = [　　　　] ml mixture

   c) 300 ml windscreen wash + [　　　　] ml water = [　　　　] ml mixture

   d) 500 ml windscreen wash + [　　　　] ml water = [　　　　] ml mixture

L1

Study the left-hand label for the regular windscreen wash.

1 Calculate how much water you would mix with 750 ml of regular windscreen wash and the resulting total amount of mixture for:

   a) Summer use

   b) Normal use

   c) Winter use

2 How many litres of mixture could you make from a 2 litre bottle of windscreen wash for:

   a) Summer use?

   b) Normal use?

   c) Winter use?

Study the right-hand label for the concentrated windscreen wash.

3 Calculate how much water you would mix with 750 ml of concentrated windscreen wash and the resulting total amount of mixture for:

   a) Summer use

   b) Normal use

   c) Winter use

4 How many litres of mixture could you make from a 2 litre bottle of concentrated windscreen wash for:

   a) Summer use?

   b) Normal use?

   c) Winter use?

L2

Study the left-hand label for the regular windscreen wash.

1 Calculate how much windscreen wash you would need (to the nearest 10 ml) to mix with water to fill a 3000 ml reservoir for:

a) Summer use

b) Normal use

c) Winter use

2 Calculate how much windscreen wash you would need (to the nearest 10 ml) to mix with water to fill a 4000 ml reservoir for:

a) Summer use

b) Normal use

c) Winter use

Study the right-hand label for the concentrated windscreen wash.

3 Calculate how much concentrated windscreen wash you would need (to the nearest 10 ml) to mix with water to fill a 3000 ml reservoir for:

a) Summer use

b) Normal use

c) Winter use

4 Calculate how much concentrated windscreen wash you would need to mix with water to fill a 4000 ml reservoir for:

a) Summer use

b) Normal use

c) Winter use

5 Now compare the prices. If a 2000 ml bottle of regular windscreen wash costs £4 and a 2000 ml bottle of double concentrate windscreen wash costs £6, calculate which offers better value for:

a) Summer use

b) Normal use

c) Winter use

Working with whole numbers

SOURCE Converting between systems

Staff in the workshop find it useful to have information available so they can convert between the different measurement systems used by various manufacturers and suppliers. They have displayed the following information on the wall.

Approximate conversion between mm/inches

mm	inches
50	2
100	4
150	6
300	12 (= 1 foot)

Approximate conversion between miles/km

10 miles = 16 km   40 km = 25 miles

Approximate conversion between gallons/litres

10 gallons = 45 litres   50 litres = 11 gallons

Converting temperature in Fahrenheit to Celsius

$$C = \frac{5(F - 32)}{9}$$

C = degrees Celsius
F = degrees Fahrenheit

E3

1 Using the information given, convert the lengths given in mm to inches.

a) 200 mm

b) 500 mm

c) 600 mm

d) 25 mm

e) 75 mm

f) 325 mm

g) 675 mm

h) 1000 mm

i) 1200 mm

j) 1500 mm

k) 2000 mm

2 Using the information given, convert the lengths given in feet and inches to mm.

a) 10 inches

b) 5 inches

c) 1 foot 2 inches

d) 1 foot 10 inches

e) 2 feet

f) 2 feet 4 inches

g) 2 feet 10 inches

h) 3 feet

i) 5 feet

j) 6 feet

k) 6 feet 6 inches

3 A car has length 4500 mm and width 1800 mm. What are its length and width in:

a) inches?

b) feet and inches?

L1

Use the information on converting miles/km and gallons/litres to estimate the answers to the following.

1 If a car's top speed is 120 miles per hour, what is it in km per hour?

2 If a car's top speed is 125 miles per hour, what is it in km per hour?

3 If a car's top speed is 240 km per hour, what is it in miles per hour?

4 If a car's top speed is 220 km per hour, what is it in miles per hour?

5 If a car's fuel tank can hold 15 gallons, how many litres can it hold?

6 If a car's fuel tank can hold 75 litres, how many gallons can it hold?

7 If a car does 40 miles to the gallon, how many kilometres to the gallon does it do?

8 If a car does 60 miles to the gallon, how many kilometres to the gallon does it do?

9 A car does 20 km to the litre. How many miles to the litre is this?

10 Car specifications usually give the number of litres per 100 km.

a) Rewrite 20 km to the litre as the number of litres per 100 km.

b) Rewrite 25 km to the litre as the number of litres per 100 km.

L2

1 The formula for converting °F to °C is shown on the left-hand flow chart.

Starting from the bottom and reversing the operations, complete the right-hand flow chart to convert °C to °F (for example, use multiply instead of divide and add instead of subtract).

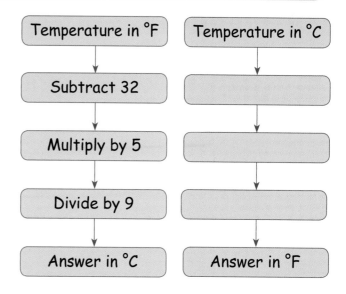

2 Use the formula on page 30 to convert the following temperatures from °F to °C.

   a) 59 °F

   b) 86 °F

   c) 32 °F

   d) 14 °F

3 Use the flow chart above to check your answers.

4 Write your flow chart as a formula and use it to convert the following temperatures from °C to °F.

   a) 20 °C

   b) 100 °C

   c) 0 °C

   d) –10 °C

5 Check your answers using the first formula or flow chart to see if your own formula is correct.

Working with fractions, decimals and percentages

Capacities – fuel tanks, engine oil, coolants and windscreen wash

Technicians at garages have to check fuel tanks, engine oil, coolants and windscreen wash. Vehicles have a range of different capacities for each.

Fuel tanks (nominal content in litres)

Car A	Car B	Car C	Car D	Car E	Car F
45	53	72	65	68	120

Engine oil with filter change (in litres)

Car A	Car B	Car C	Car D	Car E	Car F
3	3.5	4.5	4.25	4.5	5.5

Engine oil between Min and Max on the dipstick (in litres)

Car A	Car B	Car C	Car D	Car E	Car F
1	1	1	1	1	1.2

Cooling systems (in litres)

	Car A	Car B	Car C	Car D	Car E	Car F
Vehicles with manual transmission	4.9	5	6.5	6.1	5.3	7.1
Vehicles with air-conditioning	4.9	5	6.7	6.1	5.4	7.1

25% antifreeze is recommended in coolants for British winters.

E3

Study the table showing fuel tank capacities.

1   Rounding your answer to the nearest litre, how many litres of fuel are left in the tank for:

a) car A?

b) car B?

c) car D?

d) car F?

2   How many litres have been used since the tank was last filled for:

a) car C?

b) car E?

3   It costs £64 to fill a fuel tank. How much will it cost to fill the tank from:

a) $\frac{1}{4}$ full?

b) $\frac{1}{8}$ full?

4   Tick the fractions that are equivalent to $\frac{1}{4}$.

a) $\frac{3}{8}$ ☐

b) $\frac{2}{8}$ ☐

c) $\frac{2}{6}$ ☐

d) $\frac{4}{12}$ ☐

e) $\frac{3}{12}$ ☐

f) $\frac{4}{16}$ ☐

Now study the table about cooling systems.

5   Write the capacities of the cooling systems for vehicles with manual transmissions in order, start with the smallest.

6   Match the fractions, decimals and percentages.

25%		50%
$\frac{1}{2}$		$\frac{1}{4}$
0.25		0.5

7   Is it enough to put 1 litre of antifreeze into the cooling system for car A? Explain.

L1

1 Jess drives car C. She starts the day with $\frac{1}{2}$ a tank of fuel. Her first journey uses $\frac{1}{2}$ of this.

a) What fraction of a full tank has the journey used?

b) How many litres is this?

c) After the journey Jess fills the tank, paying £1.36 per litre. What is the cost?

2 A full fuel tank costs Ben £54. He makes two journeys using about $\frac{1}{4}$ and then $\frac{1}{3}$ of the tank.

a) What fraction of the tank has been used?

b) How much will Ben pay if he refills the tank with petrol at the same price per litre as before?

3 Oil is available in 5-litre cans. What fraction of the can is left after an oil change for the following?

a) car A

c) car C

b) car B

d) car D

4 Leo checks the oil level in car D.

He estimates it to be $\frac{1}{5}$ over the Min mark.

Remember: 1 litre = 1000 ml

a) How many ml over the Min mark is this?

b) What fraction of a 1-litre can of oil would be used to fill the oil to the Max mark?

5 How many litres of antifreeze is recommended in British winters for:

a) car A?

b) car C with air-conditioning?

L2

1 Yui starts the day with a full tank in car F. She makes three journeys that use about $\frac{1}{8}$, $\frac{1}{4}$ and $\frac{1}{5}$ of the tank.

   a) What fraction of the full tank has been used?

   b) How many litres is this?

2 A fuel tank is quarter full. A journey uses $\frac{1}{3}$ of this fuel. What fraction of the full tank is this?

3 Karl checks the level of oil in car F. He estimates it to be $\frac{1}{4}$ over the Min mark.

   a) How many ml over the Min mark is this?

   b) What fraction of a 2-litre can of oil would be used to fill the oil to the Max mark?

4 Jass says there's a difference of 2.1 litres between the smallest and largest coolant systems. Is he right? Explain.

5 For temperatures of –20°C, $\frac{2}{5}$ antifreeze to $\frac{3}{5}$ water is recommended for cooling systems. How many ml of antifreeze is this for:

   a) car A?

   b) car C with manual transmission?

   c) car D?

   d) car F?

6 A survey of 240 car owners showed that $\frac{1}{12}$ used a 40% mix of antifreeze to water, $\frac{3}{5}$ used a 25% mix of antifreeze to water and the rest had no antifreeze.

   a) What fraction of the survey used antifreeze?

   b) What fraction used no antifreeze?

   c) How many people used a 25% mix of antifreeze to water?

Working with fractions, decimals and percentages

 Tyre tread depths and pressures

Chris works at a garage checking, replacing and repairing tyres. She knows that careful checking of tyre pressures and tread depths is very important.

- Incorrect tyre pressure affects vehicle handling and fuel economy, and increases the wear on tyres. If the pressure is too low, the result can be tyre overheating, which could lead to tread separating or cause blow-outs at high speed.
- 2% of all fatal accidents are caused by under-inflated tyres.
- The minimum legal tread for tyres is 1.6 mm. It is recommended that tyres be replaced when they are worn to a depth of 2–3 mm or 4 mm in winter.
- Manufacturers recommend appropriate tyres for different vehicles to match the wheel diameter, the belt type, the tyre width and depth, and speed. Below are recommended tyres and pressures for various engines in Vauxhall and Ford Focus cars.
- The same tread depth should be fitted on each axle.
- If tyres are wearing unevenly, the car steering alignment should be checked.

Tyre pressure in bar/pounds per square inch (psi)					
		Tyre pressure for load of up to 3 persons		Tyre pressure for full load	
Engine	**Tyres**	**Front (bar/psi)**	**Rear (bar/psi)**	**Front (bar/psi)**	**Rear (bar/psi)**
Vauxhall Z14 XEP	175/70 R14 185/60 R15 205/50 R16 205/45 R17	2.4/35	2.2/32	2.6/38	3.0/44
Vauxhall Z16 XEP	185/60 R15 205/50 R16 205/45 R17	2.4/35	2.2/32	2.6/38	3.0/44
Vauxhall Z16 LET	185/55 R16 195/50 R16 205/50 R16 205/45 R17	2.8/41	2.6/38	3.0/44	3.4/49
Vauxhall Z17 DTH	185/60 R15 205/50 R16 205/45 R17	2.6/38	2.4/35	2.8/41	3.2/46
Ford Focus: all models	185/65 R14	2.2/32	2.2/32	2.3/34	3.1/46
	195/55 R15	2.0/29	2.0/29	2.2/32	3.1/46
	125/80 R15	4.2/62	4.2/62	4.2/62	4.2/62

> **Remember:**
> 1 bar = 14.5 psi

E3

1 The depth of tread in mm is checked at different places across the tyre and recorded during the MOT test. For example:

Left side of tyre	Middle of tyre	Right side of tyre
1.6	1.6	1.7

The depth of tread in the middle of the tyre is used to decide whether the tread is legal or illegal. For each tyre in the table below, select the depth of tread in the middle of the tyre. Record the depth in the middle of the tyre and whether it is legal or illegal.

Tyre tread depths in mm			
	Left side of tyre	Middle of tyre	Right side of tyre
Nearside front	2.0	1.5	1.8
Nearside rear	2.5	2.5	2.4
Offside front	1.4	1.5	1.5
Offside rear	1.6	1.6	1.7

		Lowest depth	Middle depth	Legal/ illegal
a)	Nearside front			
b)	Nearside rear			
c)	Offside front			
d)	Offside rear			

2 Technicians recommend replacing tyres where the tread is worn.

   a) At what depth will a technician suggest replacing a tyre during spring, summer or autumn?

   b) At what depth will a technician suggest replacing a tyre during winter?

3 A technician measures the tyre treads on eight tyres. He records:

   | 3.8 mm   4.9 mm   2.1 mm   2.6 mm   3.7 mm   5 mm   6.3 mm   4.2 mm |

   a) For which treads would you recommend replacing tyres in summer?

   b) For which treads would you recommend replacing tyres in winter?

4 A technician puts new tyres on a Vauxhall with a Z16 XEP engine. Which tyre pressures are correct, too high or too low?

   a) Front tyres   2.2

   b) Rear tyres   2.4

L1

1 A technician measures tyre tread for MOT tests. He checks the depth of tread in mm at different places across each tyre and records the measurements. For example:

Left side of tyre	Middle of tyre	Right side of tyre
1.6	1.6	1.7

The depth of tread in the middle of the tyre is used to decide whether the tread is legal or illegal. For each tyre in the table below, record the depth of tread in the middle of the tyre, say whether the tread is over or under the legal limit, and record by how much.

Tyre tread depths in mm			
	Left side of tyre	Middle of tyre	Right side of tyre
Nearside front	1.5	1.5	1.6
Nearside rear	2.7	2.8	2.8
Offside front	1.1	1.0	0.9
Offside rear	3.4	3.3	3.2

	Lowest depth	Legal/ illegal	mm over/ under legal limit
a) Nearside front			
b) Nearside rear			
c) Offside front			
d) Offside rear			

2 For each engine, say by how much the tyre pressure needs to be increased when there is a heavy load.

Vauxhall engine	For up to 3 people		For a full load	
	Front tyre	Rear tyre	Increase front tyre by	Increase rear tyre by
Z14 XEP	2.4/35	2.2/32		
Z16 LET	2.8/41	2.6/38		
Z17 DTH	2.6/38	2.4/35		

3 For each engine, say by how much the tyre pressure needs to be decreased when returning tyre pressure to normal load.

Engine	For up to 3 people		For a full load	
	Decrease front tyre by	Decrease rear tyre by	Front tyre	Rear tyre
Vauxhall Z16 XEP			2.6/38	3.0/44
Ford 185/65 R14			2.3/34	3.1/46
Ford 195/55 R15			2.2/32	3.1/46

4 What recommendations would you make for a car with four similar tyres with the following tread depths: front 3.1 mm and 2.6 mm, rear 3.3 mm and 2.7 mm? Explain why.

L2

1   Before his winter holiday, Jay checks his tyres, including the spare. He says two are illegal, one has double the required tread depth, one has over three times the required depth and the other nearly four times the required depth.

a) Give possible tread depths for all five of his tyres.

b) As well as getting two new legal tyres, what other advice would you give Jay?

2   Tyres on a car have the following tyre pressures in bar. What are the equivalent psi values? Round up to the next whole number.

a) 4.0

b) 3.5

c) 2.7

d) 3.8

e) 4.6

3   The following table gives the number of fatal road accidents between 2001 and 2010. Using the data on page 38, complete the table to show the numbers that can be attributed to under-inflated tyres.

Reported fatal road casualties										
Year	2001	2002	2003	2004	2005	2006	2007	2008	2009	2010
Fatalities	3450	3431	3508	3221	3201	3172	2946	2538	2222	1850
Caused by tyres										

4   What are the three most important points about tyres that you would give a new driver?

Working with fractions, decimals and percentages

 **Car emissions**

European legislation requires manufacturers to make new cars that give fewer emissions. Car tax is based on the carbon dioxide (CO_2) emissions of the vehicle and tax is cheaper for 'greener' cars to encourage motorists to buy cars with fewer emissions. Here are some facts about car emissions.

Table A: Vehicles registered on or after 1 March 2001 (diesel or petrol)

Tax band	CO_2 emissions (g/km)	Tax for 12 months	Tax for 6 months
A	Up to 100	£0	Not available
B	101–110	£20.00	Not available
C	111–120	£30.00	Not available
D	121–130	£100.00	£55.00
E	131–140	£120.00	£66.00
F	141–150	£135.00	£74.25
G	151–165	£170.00	£93.50
H	166–175	£195.00	£107.25
I	176–185	£215.00	£118.25
J	186–200	£250.00	£137.50
K	201–225	£270.00	£148.50
L	226–255	£460.00	£253.00
M	Over 255	£475.00	£261.25

Table B: Average CO_2 emissions for new cars, 2000–2011

2000	2010	2011
181 g/km	144.2 g/km	138.1 g/km

Table C: Share of new car market with CO_2 emissions

CO_2 emissions	2000	2010	2011
up to 100 g/km	0.0%	1.8%	3.4%
up to 130 g/km	0.9%	38.2%	46.8%
up to 140 g/km	8.2%	56.5%	65%

Table D: New cars on the market, 2000–2011

	2000	2010	2011
Total number of new cars	2 221 647	2 030 846	1 941 253
Diesel	14.1%	46.1%	50.6%
Alternatively-fuelled	0.0%	1.1%	1.3%

Remember:
g/km = grams per kilometre; Mt CO_2 = million tonnes of carbon dioxide.

Table E: Cars in use in the UK, 2000–2010

	2000	2009	2010
Total CO_2 emissions from all cars in use	75.1 Mt CO_2	69.7 Mt CO_2	67.4 Mt CO_2
Total number of cars in use	27.8 million	31.0 million	31.3 million

E3

1 Look at table A.

a) How much is 12 months of tax for a car in band D?

b) How much is 6 months of tax for a car in band D?

c) Which is the better buy – 6 months' tax or 12 months' tax? Explain your reasoning.

2 Debbie says $\frac{1}{4}$ of the tax bands don't offer a 6-month option. Kim disagrees. Who is right? Explain.

3 Match the fractions and percentage values.

20%

a) $\frac{1}{2}$ 50%

b) $\frac{1}{4}$ 10%

c) $\frac{1}{10}$ 25%

33%

4 Look at table C. Answer true or false.

a) Fewer than $\frac{1}{10}$ had emissions under 130g/km in 2000. True ☐ False ☐

b) Under $\frac{1}{2}$ had emissions under 130g/km in 2010. True ☐ False ☐

c) Over $\frac{1}{2}$ had emissions under 140g/km in 2010. True ☐ False ☐

d) Just under $\frac{1}{2}$ had emissions under 130g/km in 2011. True ☐ False ☐

e) Over $\frac{1}{10}$ had emissions under 100g/km in 2011. True ☐ False ☐

5 Look at table D. In which year did $\frac{1}{2}$ the new cars have diesel engines?

6 Max says $\frac{1}{10}$ of the new cars sold were alternatively fuelled in 2011. Is this right? Explain.

L1

1 Look at the tax for 12 months on table A.

Answer true or false.

a) Tax band C is $\frac{1}{4}$ of band E.　　　　True ☐　　　False ☐

b) Tax band B is $\frac{1}{5}$ of band D.　　　　True ☐　　　False ☐

c) Tax band D is $\frac{5}{6}$ of band E.　　　　True ☐　　　False ☐

d) Tax band E is $\frac{1}{2}$ of band F.　　　　True ☐　　　False ☐

e) Tax band K is 200% of band F.　　　True ☐　　　False ☐

f) Tax band D is $\frac{2}{5}$ of band J.　　　　True ☐　　　False ☐

g) Tax band C is $\frac{1}{3}$ of band D.　　　　True ☐　　　False ☐

2 Look at table C.

What percentage of the new car market had CO_2 emissions:

a) between 100 and 130 g/km in 2010?

b) between 100 and 130 g/km in 2011?

c) between 130 and 140 g/km in 2010?

d) between 130 and 140 g/km in 2011?

Study table D.

3 What percentage of the new car market was fuelled by petrol in:

a) 2000?

b) 2010?

c) 2011?

Round the figures in the table on page 42 to the nearest whole percentage.

4 Estimate the number of new cars fuelled by diesel in:

a) 2000

b) 2010

c) 2011

5 Estimate the number of new cars fuelled by alternative fuel in:

a) 2010

b) 2011

L2

1 Look at table B. What was the percentage reduction of average CO_2 emissions in new cars:

a) between 2000 and 2010?

b) between 2010 and 2011?

2 Look at table D. How many more new cars were alternatively fuelled in 2011 than in 2010?

3 Look at tables A and C. How many new cars cost between £20 and £100 for 12 months' tax in:

a) 2000?

b) 2010?

c) 2011?

4 Look at table E. Find the percentage reduction in total CO_2 emissions from all cars in use:

a) between 2000 and 2009

b) between 2009 and 2010

5 Find the percentage increase/decrease in the total number of cars in use:

a) between 2000 and 2009.

b) between 2009 and 2010.

6 EU targets for manufacturers aim for 65% of new cars to have emissions of 130 g/km in 2012, 75% by 2013, 80% by 2014 and 100% by 2015.

Do you think this might be achieved? Explain.

Working with fractions, decimals and percentages

SOURCE Choosing takeaways

A garage is located near a number of takeaway businesses. The technicians have collected these takeaway menus.

Menu 1

10% off for collection in addition to other offers

Set menu for 2   £18

Special Offer
12% off set menu

Prawn crackers
Chicken soup
Sweet and sour chicken
Yung chow fried rice

Main menu

Barbecued spare ribs £4.35
Sweet and sour pork.................................... £4.20
Szechuan beef... £4.20
Crispy chicken with beansprouts £4.50
Beef chop suey £3.90
Special fried rice £3.60
Steamed or fried rice £1.80

$\frac{1}{3}$ **off main menu orders before 6:30pm**

Chinese House

Menu 2

Balti Corner

Balti specialities

10% off for collection

	Meat	Prawn	Veg
Balti	£4.90	£7.30	£4.40
Dhansak	£5.30	£7.20	£4.30
Dopiaza	£5.20	£7.40	£4.50
Biryani	£6.50	£7.90	£4.70

Popular curry dishes

15% off for collection

	Meat	Prawn	Veg
Curry	£4.80	£5.60	£4.60
Jalfrezi	£5.20	£5.70	£4.30
Tikka	£5.90	£6.10	£4.20

Fried or pilau rice £1.99
Nan bread £1.50

10% off for collection in addition to other offers

Menu 3

Burger and Pizza House

20% off meal deals

5% off all pizzas

15% of all side orders

Mega Meal Deal

Large, med & small pizza
Potato wedges, coleslaw, salad, fries, 2 dips, drink   **£19.95**

Family Meal Deal

Large, med pizza
10 chicken wings, salad, fries, garlic bread, 2 dips, drink   **£14.95**

Bumper Burger Deal

4 burgers, wedges, sweetcorn, dips, drink   **£12.50**

Side orders

Wedges   **£1.50**
Coleslaw   **90p**
Sweetcorn   **95p**

Pizzas

Large pizza + 3 toppings   **£8.99**
Med pizza + 3 toppings   **£5.99**
Small pizza + 3 toppings   **£4.50**

E3

1   The technicians would like to order these meals from Chinese House:

They order before 6.30 pm but are not going to collect. Find the discount, in money, and the cost, with discount, for each item.

1 × beef chop suey
1 × crispy chicken with beansprouts
1 × szechuan beef
1 × special fried rice
1 × fried rice

a) Beef chop suey

Discount [   ]   Cost [   ]

b) Crispy chicken with beansprouts

Discount [   ]   Cost [   ]

c) Szechuan beef

Discount [   ]   Cost [   ]

d) Special fried rice

Discount [   ]   Cost [   ]

e) Fried rice

Discount [   ]   Cost [   ]

f) What will the food cost in total?

[   ]

2   Tim finds a different discount from Chinese House. You can buy two meals and get the cheapest one at half price. All rice dishes have a quarter off the price. These discounts cannot be used with any other offers.

a) Which meal will be half price? [   ]

b) What will it cost with this discount on the full price? [   ]

c) What will the two rice dishes cost? [   ]

d) What will the food cost in total? [   ]

3   Which discount would you recommend? Explain why.

L1

1   Eight technicians would like to order curries.

Fill in the table to show 10% of the price of each Balti meal and the discounted cost.

Remember: 10% = 10p in every £ or divide by 10.

		Meat	Prawn	Veg
Balti	10% of price			
	cost			
Dhansak	10% of price			
	cost			
Dopiaza	10% of price			
	cost			
Biryani	10% of price			
	cost			

2   Fill in the table to show 15% of the price of each curry and the discounted cost.

Remember: you can find 10% and then 5%, and then add them together to make 15%.

		Meat	Prawn	Veg
Curry	15% of price			
	cost			
Jalfrezi	15% of price			
	cost			
Tikka	15% of price			
	cost			

3   Explain another way of finding the cost with a 15% reduction.

4   There is a budget of £35. Choose eight curries that will fit in the budget. What do they cost?

L2

1 World Cup football is on. The technicians decide to have a takeaway while they watch the match. They have three options and plan to collect the meals before 6.30 pm:

- Chinese House: the set menu for two, barbecued spare ribs, crispy chicken with beansprouts, sweet and sour pork and two portions of fried rice.
- Balti Corner: meat balti, veg biryani, veg dopiaza, prawn jalfrezi, meat tikka, three nan breads and two portions of pilau rice.
- Bumper Burger House: mega meal deal, a separate medium pizza, 2 wedges and 2 portions of sweetcorn.

What is the cost for the meal from:

a) Chinese House?

b) Balti Corner?

c) Bumper Burger and Pizza House?

d) Which would you recommend? Explain why.

2 What fraction of the price of the large pizza is:

a) the price of the medium pizza?

b) the price of the small pizza?

3 What fraction of the cost of the mega meal deal is:

a) the family meal deal?

b) the bumper burger deal?

Measures, shape and space

Calculating time

 FOCUS ON Reading the date and time

Read dates in different formats

Watch out for the different ways of writing the date. The order is not always the same.

In Britain the day comes first, then the month:

- 4/1/12 = 4 January 2012
- 1/4/12 = 1 April 2012.

In America the month is written first:

- 1/4/12 = January 4 2012
- 4/1/12 = April 1 2012.

Reading and recording time

am and pm

We use **am** and **pm** to split the day into two halves.

- am starts at midnight, 12am, and goes through the night and morning until midday.
- pm starts at midday, 12pm, and goes though the afternoon and evening until midnight.

24-hour clock

Instead of using am and pm, the hours are numbered up to 24 on the 24-hour clock. For pm times add on 12 hours.

You need to write the time on the 24-hour clock using four digits. Add a leading zero if needed. For example:

- 07:30 = 7:30am

Note that two dots (a colon) separate the hours from the minutes. Some timetables miss the colon out.

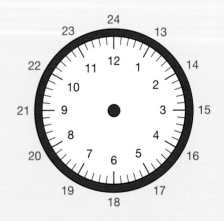

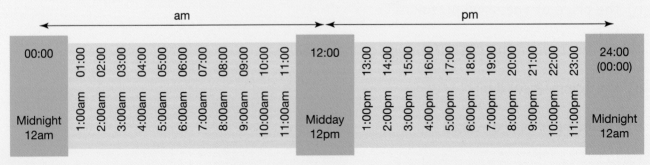

Adding and subtracting hours, minutes and seconds

Remember: 60 seconds = 1 minute; 60 minutes = 1 hour

---

40 seconds + $1\frac{1}{2}$ minutes

minutes	seconds
	40 +
1	30
1	70

70 seconds = 1 minute 10 seconds

1 minute + 1 minute + 10 seconds
= 2 minutes 10 seconds

---

3 hours 24 minutes – 55 minutes

3 hours 24 minutes = 2 hours + 24 minutes + 60 minutes (1 hour)

hours	minutes
2	84 –
	55
2	29

2 hours 29 minutes

Calculating lengths of time: adding on

How much time is there between 10:45 and 12:30?

		hours	minutes
Start time	10:45		
Number of minutes to next hour	10:45 → 11:00		15 +
Number of hours	11:00 → 12:00	1	
Number of minutes after the hour	12:00 → 12:30		30
		1	45

Calculating lengths of time: subtracting

How long is it between 8:15am and 2:45pm?

Put into 24-hour clock time, end time first   14:45 –
08:15

6:30 = 6 hours 30 minutes

Measuring length, weight and capacity

 FOCUS ON Reading scales and measuring

Making quick estimates

You can estimate some measurements quickly by using things you know. You can also use these methods to consider whether an answer you have calculated or measured is reasonable.

- 1 millimetre (mm) is about the width of this full stop (•).
- 1 centimetre (cm) is probably about the width of your little finger.
- 1 metre (m) is probably about the length from your nose to the tips of your fingers.
- 1 gram (g) is about the weight of 10 matchsticks.
- 1 kilogram (kg) is the weight of most bags of sugar.
- 1 litre (l) is the quantity of liquid in most bottles of squash or cartons of juice.

> Check the units on the ruler and always start reading the scale from zero.

Using a ruler

A ruler is a type of scale.
This ruler measures in centimetres (cm)
and millimetres (mm).

- 10 mm = 1 cm

- The nail measures 20 mm or 2 cm.

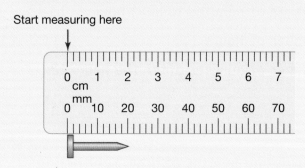

Start measuring here

Reading labelled and unlabelled measures

It's easy to read off some measurements on a scale – they are labelled, as on this scale that you might find on a measuring jug.

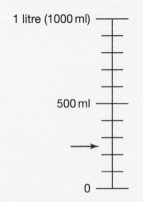

To read off measurements at marked divisions, you need to work out what each division represents. Read two labelled divisions and find the difference. For example:

$$1000 \text{ ml} - 500 \text{ ml} = 500 \text{ ml}$$

Divide by the number of divisions from one labelled mark to the next:

$$500 \text{ ml} \div 5 = 100 \text{ ml}$$

On this scale each division is 100 ml.

To read off measurements that are not marked, you need to estimate the distance along the scale between one marked division and the next.

On this scale the arrow points to about halfway between two marked divisions. The unlabelled divisions are 100 ml apart and the arrow points to $2\frac{1}{2}$ divisions up. So the measurement is 250 ml.

Reading measures in decimal format

Look at the position of the numbers and the decimal point (.). Note whether a number is in the tenths column or the hundredths column. For example:

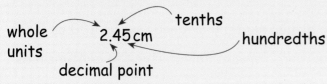

whole
units
2.45 cm

tenths

hundredths

decimal point

Ask yourself: What is the value of
one-tenth or one-hundredth of the unit?

Metres and centimetres

Units	Decimal point	Tenths	Hundredths
1 metre	.	$\frac{1}{10}$ metre	$\frac{1}{100}$ metre
100 cm	.	10 cm	1 cm

Example:

2.45 m

= 200 cm + 40 cm + 5 cm

= 2 m 45 cm or 245 cm

> Make sure you always calculate using the same units.

Kilograms and grams

Units	Decimal point	Tenths	Hundredths	Thousandths
1 kg	.	$\frac{1}{10}$ kg	$\frac{1}{100}$ kg	$\frac{1}{1000}$ kg
1000 g	.	100 g	10 g	1 g

You can use the same principle for litres and millilitres.

Calculating measures in decimal format

When adding or subtracting measures with decimals, make sure you line the numbers up with the decimal points under each other.

Example:

1 kilogram + 150 grams + 75 g = 1 . 0 kg

    0.1 5 0 kg
+   0.0 7 5 kg
=   1.2 2 5 kg

FOCUS ON Converting measures

Converting between metric measures

To convert between metric measures you need to either multiply or divide by 10, 100 or 1000.

Think about the direction in which you are converting, for example metres to centimetres or centimetres to metres.

Always ask yourself: Would I expect the answer to be larger or smaller than what I started with?

Converting lengths

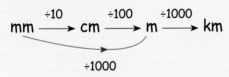

Converting capacity

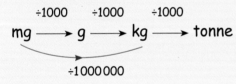

Converting weight

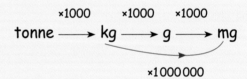

Imperial measures

Remember these quick approximations.

- 1 inch is about the size of a thumb from the knuckle to the end of the nail.

- 1 foot is about the length of many rulers.

- 1 yard is a little shorter than a metre, which is about the length from your nose to the end of your fingers when you stretch your arm out.

- 2 lb (2 pounds) is slightly less than most bags of sugar and 1 lb (1 pound) is slightly less than a small tub of engine grease.

- $1\frac{3}{4}$ pints is the quantity of liquid in most cartons of juice or small bottles of engine oil.

- Most standard car batteries weigh between 3 and 4 stone.

Converting imperial measures

Converting between imperial measures involves more numbers than with metric measures. You may need to make two calculations.

Also remember you cannot use a decimal point as you can with metric measures.

Example:

How many yards is 54 inches?

Inches are smaller than yards.
We expect fewer yards, so divide.

> **Remember:**
> 12 inches = 1 foot
> 3 feet = 1 yard

54 ÷ 12 (to find feet) = 4 feet, remainder 6 inches

4 ÷ 3 (to find yards) = 1 yard, remainder 1 foot

Answer = 1 yard + 1 foot + 6 inches or 1 yard and 18 inches, but not 1.18 yards.

Converting between metric and imperial measures

Consider whether you need to divide or multiply for the conversion.

Example:

How many inches is 10 cm?

10 ÷ 2.54 = 4 inches

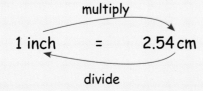

multiply

1 inch   =   2.54 cm

divide

> **Remember:**
> • 1 in = 2.54 cm
> • 10 mm = 1 cm
> • 1 oz = 28.35 g
> • 1 lb = 0.454 kg
> • 1000 g = 1 kg

Example:

How many centimetres is 10 inches?

10 × 2.54 = 25.4 cm

Perimeter, area and scale drawings

 FOCUS ON Measuring areas and volume, and using scale ratios

Area

An area, such as the floor of a room or the expanse of a motor vehicle workshop, is measured in square units. The measurement is written with a symbol to show it is squared, for example m² or cm².

The formula is:

Area = length × width or A = l × w

Always use the same units in a calculation, for example:

1.1 m × 0.8 m or 110 cm × 80 cm

When converting from m² to cm², remember to convert the units for both the length and the width measurements.

1 m² = 1 m [1 m square] = 100 cm [100 cm square] = 10 000 cm²

Perimeter

If you measure the distance all the way round a shape, you have measured the perimeter. For example, the perimeter of a simple shape like a rectangle is two lengths and two widths.

The formula is:

Perimeter = 2 × (length + width) or P = 2 (l + w)

Always use the same units in a calculation, for example:

2 × (110 cm + 60 cm) or 2 × (1.1 m + 0.6 m)

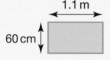

Area of a circle

The formula is:

Area = π × radius × radius or A = πr²

> **Remember:** π is often rounded to 3.14, but you can also use the function on your calculator.
>
> Don't confuse πr² and 2πr.
>
> **Remember:** you need *squared* units for area.

Circumference

The perimeter of a circle is called the circumference.

The formula is:

Circumference = π × diameter or C = πd

Or **Circumference = 2 × π × radius or C = 2πr**

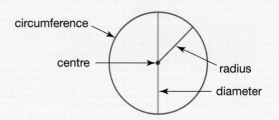

Volume

Volume is measured in cubic units. The measurement is written with a symbol to show it is cubed, for example cm^3.

The formula for the volume of a cuboid is:

Volume = length × width × height or V = l × w × h

Always use the same units in a calculation.

If converting between units, remember to consider the conversion for all three dimensions.

$1 m^3 = $ ⬡ $100 cm × 100 cm × 100 cm = 1000000 cm^3$

> **Remember:** convert volume to litres using 1 litre = $1000 cm^3$.

Using scale ratios

Maps and scale drawings represent real-life measurements at a smaller, specified scale.

For example, a scale of 1:20 on a plan means that the actual measurements are 20 times those on the plan. So if a measurement on a plan is 5 cm, the measurement in reality is 20 times bigger.

5 × 20 = 100 cm (1 m) in reality.

In this case, the ratio of 5 cm to 1 m can be written as 1:20.

To calculate the ratio of 4 cm to 1 km, make the units the same and then simplify the ratio (if possible). For example:

4 cm : 1 km = 4 cm : 1 × 1000 × 100
              = 4 : 100000
              = 1 : 25000 (the scale of
                   some Ordnance Survey maps)

> **Remember:** 1 km = 1000 m and 1 m = 100 cm.

Drawing plans and maps

If the scale of a plan or map is 1 : n (where n is a number), divide the actual distances by n to give the corresponding distance on the map or plan.

> **Remember:** it is more convenient to work in cm for lengths on a plan or map.

Calculating time

SOURCE — Car number plates

Simon finds it useful to know how old a car is when he is working on it, particularly as he specialises in restoring classic cars.

Current number plates

Local memory tag — **BD51 SMR** — Random element

Age identifier

The current number plate format was introduced in 2001.

The first two letters show where the vehicle was registered.

The two numbers in the middle show the age of the vehicle down to a six-month period from March to August or from September to February (see the table).

The last three letters are random and give the car a unique identity.

Age identifiers		
Year	**1 March to end August**	**1 September to end February**
2001/02	01	51
2002/03	02	52
2003/04	03	53
2004/05	04	54
2005/06	05	55
2006/07	06	56
2007/08	07	57
2008/09	08	58
2009/10	09	59
2010/11	10	60
2011/12	11	61
2012/13	12	62
	and so on	until 50/00 in 2050/51

Earlier number plate formats

The old prefix system, with a leading single letter to show the year of first registration, began on 1 August 1983.

Before this, letters were used as a suffix. The following table shows both systems.

Suffix letter (at end of registration)			
Jan 1963 to Dec 1963	A	Aug 1973 to July 1974	M
Jan 1964 to Dec 1964	B	Aug 1974 to July 1975	N
Jan 1965 to Dec 1965	C	Aug 1975 to July 1976	P
Jan 1966 to Dec 1966	D	Aug 1976 to July 1977	R
Jan 1967 to July 1967	E	Aug 1977 to July 1978	S
Aug 1967 to July 1968	F	Aug 1978 to July 1979	T
Aug 1968 to July 1969	G	Aug 1979 to July 1980	V
Aug 1969 to July 1970	H	Aug 1980 to July 1981	W
Aug 1970 to July 1971	J	Aug 1981 to July 1982	X
Aug 1971 to July 1972	K	Aug 1982 to July 1983	Y
Aug 1972 to July 1973	L		

Prefix letter (at start of registration)			
A	Aug 1983 to July 1984	M	Aug 1994 to July 1995
B	Aug 1984 to July 1985	N	Aug 1995 to July 1996
C	Aug 1985 to July 1986	P	Aug 1996 to July 1997
D	Aug 1986 to July 1987	R	Aug 1997 to July 1998
E	Aug 1987 to July 1988	S	Aug 1998 to Feb 1999
F	Aug 1988 to July 1989	T	Mar 1999 to Aug 1999
G	Aug 1989 to July 1990	V	Sep 1999 to Feb 2000
H	Aug 1990 to July 1991	W	Mar 2000 to Aug 2000
J	Aug 1991 to July 1992	X	Sep 2000 to Feb 2001
K	Aug 1992 to July 1993	Y	Mar 2001 to Aug 2001
L	Aug 1993 to July 1994		

On a car with a private registration the age can be determined using the Vehicle Identification Number (V.I.N.).

E3

1 If cars with the following registrations were brought into the garage in May 2013, how old were they to the nearest year?

a) VB12DWG

e) RD07NAP

b) WA09TCL

f) FM04FPC

c) GK03KPH

g) VB08RFS

d) GK10FRD

h) FM11MCL

2 If cars with the following registrations were brought into the garage in December 2013, how old were they to the nearest year?

a) GT60WKJ

e) GK56XDR

b) WN57BRS

f) WA51YNK

c) VR52DFP

g) RD61HRM

d) WN59LNA

h) GT54SBF

3 If a car was registered in the month and year shown below, what two digits would be in the middle of the number plate?

a) May 2007

b) January 2008

c) October 2009

d) June 2013

e) December 2011

f) June 2011

g) January 2005

h) November 2013

L1

1   If a car was registered in the month and year shown below, what would the suffix or prefix be?

a) September 1978

b) September 1997

c) June 1983

d) December 1972

e) February 2000

f) April 1965

g) January 1993

h) August 1969

i) May 1980

j) October 1975

k) March 1990

l) November 1965

m) July 1999

n) August 1972

o) December 1984

p) June 1964

2   If old and classic cars with the following suffixes and prefixes were brought into the garage in January 2014, approximately how many years old would they be?

a) Suffix E

b) Prefix E

c) Suffix J

d) Prefix D

e) Suffix X

f) Prefix F

g) Prefix A

h) Suffix A

L2

1 Calculate the maximum and minimum age difference to the nearest half year between cars with the following registration features.

	Car 1	Car 2	Maximum age difference	Minimum age difference
a)	Middle digits 51	Middle digits 12		
b)	Prefix V	Middle digits 60		
c)	Prefix N	Middle digits 10		
d)	Prefix F	Middle digits 62		
e)	Prefix K	Prefix X		
f)	Prefix A	Prefix S		
g)	Suffix L	Suffix S		
h)	Suffix F	Suffix W		
i)	Suffix P	Prefix E		
j)	Suffix G	Prefix G		
k)	Suffix B	Middle digits 08		
l)	Suffix A	Middle digits 62		

2 What would the middle digits be of a car registered in:

a) June 2028?

b) November 2033?

c) January 2040?

3 What would the maximum difference in age be between cars with middle digits 11 and 69?

Calculating time

SOURCE Time sheets

The mechanics at Glover's Car Works work various hours, sometimes coming in early or staying late to get jobs finished. Their start, finish and break times are recorded. Their standard working week is 37 hours, not including breaks. This is averaged out over the weeks.

Gordon Jones – Employee number 253				
Monday	**Tuesday**	**Wednesday**	**Thursday**	**Friday**
Starts 8:00am	Starts 7:30am	Starts 8:30am	Starts 8:15am	Starts 8:30am
Stops 11:00am	Stops 10:30am	Stops 11:00am	Stops 10:45am	Stops 11:00am
Starts 11:30am	Starts 11:00am	Starts 11:30am	Starts 11:15am	Starts 11:30am
Stops 1:00pm	Stops 1:00pm	Stops 1:30pm	Stops 1:15pm	Stops 3:00pm
Starts 1:45pm	Starts 1:30pm	Starts 2:15pm	Starts 1:45pm	
Stops 4:45pm	Stops 4:00pm	Stops 5:15pm	Stops 4:45pm	

Abdul Patel – Employee number 278				
Monday	**Tuesday**	**Wednesday**	**Thursday**	**Friday**
Starts 7:45am	Starts 7:30am	Starts 7:30am	Starts 7:30am	Starts 7:30am
Stops 10:15am	Stops 10:15am	Stops 10:00am	Stops 10:45am	Stops 10:00am
Starts 10:45am	Starts 10:45am	Starts 10:30am	Starts 11:15am	Starts 10:30am
Stops 1:15pm	Stops 1:15pm	Stops 1:15pm	Stops 1:45pm	Stops 1:00pm
Starts 2:00pm	Starts 1:45pm	Starts 2:00pm	Starts 2:15pm	
Stops 5:00pm	Stops 5:00pm	Stops 4:45pm	Stops 5:00pm	

Becky Phillips – Employee number 262				
Monday	**Tuesday**	**Wednesday**	**Thursday**	**Friday**
Starts 8:20am	Starts 7:40am	Starts 7:40am	Starts 7:50am	Starts 7:40am
Stops 10:30am	Stops 10:30am	Stops 10:15am	Stops 10:30am	Stops 10:30am
Starts 11:00am	Starts 11:00am	Starts 10:45am	Starts 11:00am	Starts 11:00am
Stops 1:40pm	Stops 1:15pm	Stops 1:30pm	Stops 1:30pm	Stops 1:40pm
Starts 2:15pm	Starts 2:00pm	Starts 2:00pm	Starts 2:15pm	
Stops 5:00pm	Stops 5:10pm	Stops 4:40pm	Stops 4:45pm	

E3

Study Gordon's time sheet and answer the following questions.

1 Calculate how many hours Gordon worked on each day. For each day, calculate the hours in each of the following relevant periods to fill out the tables below. Then calculate the total for each day.

a) From starting work to the start of his first break

b) From the end of his first break to the start of his second break (note that on Friday this is the end of his working day)

c) From the end of his second break to the end of the day

d) Total hours worked in the day

Monday	
a)	
b)	
c)	
d) **Total**	

Tuesday	
a)	
b)	
c)	
d) **Total**	

Wednesday	
a)	
b)	
c)	
d) **Total**	

Thursday	
a)	
b)	
c)	
d) **Total**	

Friday	
a)	
b)	
c)	
d) **Total**	

2 Calculate how many hours Gordon worked in total that week.

Study Abdul's time sheet and answer the following questions.

1 Calculate how many hours Abdul worked on Monday. Show your workings.

2 Calculate how many hours Abdul worked on Tuesday. Show your workings.

3 Calculate how many hours Abdul worked on Wednesday. Show your workings.

4 Calculate how many hours Abdul worked on Thursday. Show your workings.

5 Calculate how many hours Abdul worked on Friday. Show your workings.

6 Calculate how many hours Abdul worked that week. Show your workings.

L2

Study Becky's time sheet and answer the following questions.

1 Calculate how many hours Becky worked on Monday. Show your workings.

2 Calculate how many hours Becky worked on Tuesday. Show your workings.

3 Calculate how many hours Becky worked on Wednesday. Show your workings.

4 Calculate how many hours Becky worked on Thursday. Show your workings.

5 Calculate how many hours Becky worked on Friday. Show your workings.

6 Calculate how many hours Becky worked that week. Show your workings.

Converting measurements and calculating weights and volume

Choosing the correct tyres

It is important that employees at tyre fitters recognise the markings on tyres and the importance of fitting the correct size of tyre.

Tread wear indicators

All tyre manufacturers build a tread wear indicator into the tread pattern. This a small rubber moulding raised 1.6 mm above the base of the tread groove so that when the adjacent tread has worn down to this level it indicates the tyre should be changed. A few tyres, for example some Michelin TRX patterns, have an additional indicator at 3 mm to indicate that the tread depth is getting near the limit. Most car and light van tyres have 8 mm of tread when new.

Minimum tread depth

UK requirements are that the grooves of the tread pattern of every tyre fitted to a vehicle must be of a depth of at least 1.6 mm throughout a continuous band, comprising the central 75% of the breadth of tread and round the entire outer circumference of the tyre.

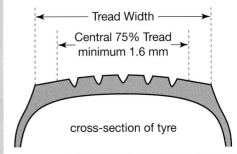

cross-section of tyre

Tyre condition

A tyre used on a vehicle or trailer must not have any cut or damage to the tread of the tyre that is more than 25 mm or 10% of the section width. Any cut or damage that it does have must not expose the cords or ply of the tyre. It must not have any internal or external lump, bulge or tear caused by separation or partial failure of the structure. If a vehicle is going to be used on the road, its tyres must be in good condition and suitable in all respects, including inflation pressure, for the use to which the vehicle is being put.

Tyre sizes

Modern tyre sizes consist of three numbers: the width of the tyre, the profile (aspect ratio) and the wheel size (these are given as a mix of metric and imperial numbers). So a tyre size of 155/70/13 is 155 mm wide, has a side wall that is 70% of the width, and fits a 13-inch wheel. The tyre size is decided by the vehicle manufacturer. More powerful cars require wider tyres to give more grip (to handle the power output and for better cornering ability). Larger cars also need bigger wheels and tyres to handle the weight of the car.

After the three numbers of the tyre size, there is usually a number and letter combination that indicates the maximum load per tyre and a certain maximum speed. The load and speed are determined by the manufacturer's design and testing based on the tyre size and tread pattern. A coarse pattern will heat up more quickly, therefore a lower speed rating will usually apply at the stated load when compared to a normal pattern.

E3

1 Mark the following measurements on the measuring tape.
The first one has been done for you.

Remember: 10 mm = 1 cm

a) 1.6 mm

b) 3 mm

c) 5 mm

d) 25 mm

2 Convert the following tyre widths to cm.

a) 150 mm

b) 140 mm

c) 170 mm

d) 270 mm

e) 210 mm

f) 190 mm

3 Mark the following tyre widths on the tape measure below.

a) 180 mm

b) 21.5 cm

c) 165 mm

d) 15.5 cm

e) 140 mm

f) 13.5 cm

g) 19 cm

h) 200 mm

4 Referring to page 66, identify from the tyres shown below:

a) the tyre with the greatest width

b) the tyre for the smallest wheel size

Tyre A

175/18/13

Tyre B

235/85/16

Tyre C

165/50/15

L1

1 Convert the following tyre widths to mm.

a) 14.5 cm [ ]   c) 21.5 cm [ ]

b) 19.5 cm [ ]   d) 26 cm [ ]

2 Referring to page 66, give the widths of the tyres below in cm.

a)

195/65/17

[ ]

c)

235/85/16

[ ]

b)

165/50/15

[ ]

d)

205/75/14

[ ]

3 The following table gives the load index and associated load weight in kg. Complete the third column by converting each weight to grams.

Load index	Weight in kg	Weight in g
0	45.0	
1	46.2	
2	47.5	
3	48.7	
4	50.0	
5	51.5	

4 The following table gives the load index and associated load weight in kg. Complete the third column by converting the weight to tonnes.

Load index	Weight in kg	Weight in tonnes
105	925	
106	950	
107	975	
108	1000	
109	1030	
110	1060	
111	1090	
112	1120	
113	1150	

Remember: 1000 kg = 1 tonne

L2

1   Convert the wheel diameters in the table below to mm using 1 inch = 25.4 mm
and calculate the overall diameter of the tyres to the nearest mm.
(Remember to double the profile height.)

Profile (mm)	Wheel diameter (in)	Wheel diameter (mm)	Overall diameter of tyre (mm)
91	14		
83	15		
90	17		
90	19		
98	22		

2   Calculate the wheel diameter in inches if:

a) the overall diameter is 602 mm and the profile is 136 mm

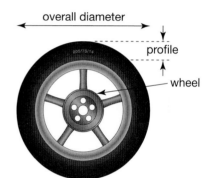

overall diameter

profile

wheel

b) the overall profile is 806 mm and the profile is 200 mm

3   The following table shows the speed symbols used on tyres, relating to the maximum
speed rating of the vehicle.

Using 1 mile = 1.6 km, complete the third column. Give your answers to the nearest km.

Speed symbol	Maximum speed capability (mph)	Maximum speed rating (km/h)
N	88	
P	94	
Q	100	
R	106	
S	113	
T	119	

4   Complete the following table by converting the maximum speed rating in km/h to mph.
Give your answer to the nearest mile.

Speed symbol	Maximum speed capability (mph)	Maximum speed rating (km/h)
U		200
V		210
W		240
VR		270
ZR		300

Converting measurements and calculating weights and volume

 **Tyre pressure**

Staff at a tyre centre need to ensure that tyre pressures are correct.

Correct tyre pressure can help to extend the life of a tyre, improve vehicle safety and maintain fuel efficiency. Pressure is measured by calculating the amount of air that has been pumped into the inner lining of the tyre in pounds per square inch (psi) or bar pressure.

Maintaining correct tyre pressure

There are three main reasons why maintaining the right tyre pressure is important.

Safety
Tyres that are under-inflated can overheat, and over-inflated tyres can lead to poor vehicle handling on the road.

Economy
Over- or under-inflated tyres suffer more damage than those with the correct pressure, and need to be replaced more frequently.
Vehicles with under-inflated tyres have increased rolling resistance and require more fuel to maintain the same speed.

Environment
Optimum fuel efficiency equates to lower CO_2 emissions.

It is important to check tyre pressure regularly. It is not always apparent that air is being lost, but it generally escapes at the rate of up to two pounds of air pressure every month. More air is usually lost during warm weather, so more frequent checks are needed when temperatures rise.

E3

1   What is each small division worth on the psi scale?

[   ]

2   What is the psi reading on each of these pressure gauges?

a) [   ]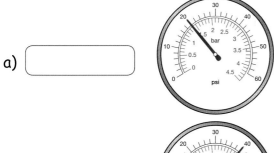

b) [   ]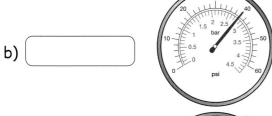

c) [   ]

d) [   ]

e) [   ]

f) [   ]

3   Mark where the needle would point on the gauge for the following psi readings.

a) 30 psi

b) 36 psi

c) 26 psi

d) 39 psi

e) 42 psi

f) 17 psi

L1

1   What is each small division worth on the bar scale?

2   What is the bar reading on each of these pressure gauges?

a)

d)

b)

e)

c)

f)

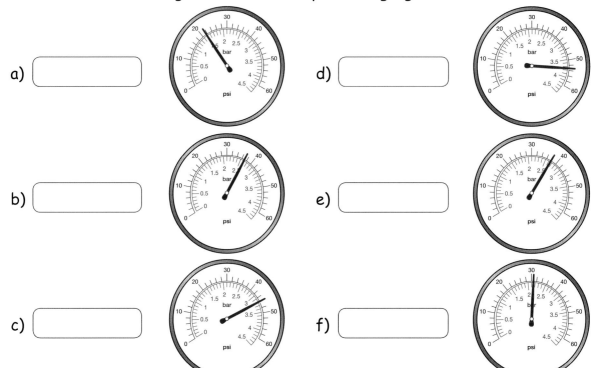

3   Mark where the needle would point on the gauge for the following bar readings.

a) 2.5 bar

d) 4.15 bar

b) 2.75 bar

e) 2.25 bar

c) 3.9 bar

f) 1.95 bar

L2

1   The tyre pressures of various car tyres were taken and the psi readings are shown below. The recommended value for each tyre is also shown. Calculate how much over or under the recommended value the reading on each gauge is.

a) Recommended
   value 23 psi

b) Recommended
   value 42 psi

c) Recommended
   value 37 psi

d) Recommended
   value 37 psi

e) Recommended
   value 31 psi

f) Recommended
   value 50 psi

2   This time when tyre pressures were taken, bar readings were recorded. The recommended value for each tyre is also shown. Calculate how much over or under the recommended value the reading on the gauge is.

a) Recommended
   value 2.4 bar

b) Recommended
   value 3.6 bar

c) Recommended
   value 3.1 bar

d) Recommended
   value 2.75 bar

e) Recommended
   value 3.2 bar

f) Recommended
   value 2.9 bar

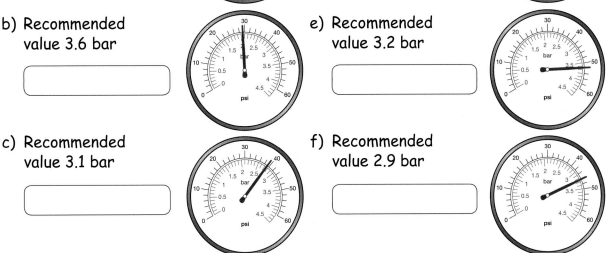

Shape and volume

 **SOURCE** Storing used oil

All garages need to ensure that they follow the guidelines and regulations below for the storage of used oil. The manager of a new garage is reviewing the information, as he needs to purchase suitable containers for his new premises.

ENVIRONMENT AGENCY
Pollution prevention guidelines

Safe storage and disposal of used oils

These guidelines are intended to help everyone who handles used oils – from people carrying out a single engine oil change to large industrial users. Compliance with these guidelines will help to reduce the risk of oil pollution of surface waters, groundwater, sewers and drains.

Garages and workshops

Sites such as garages can generate large quantities of used oil. This must be collected by a registered waste carrier or, as an alternative in England and Wales, it may be feasible to use it as a fuel for heating. This will require adequate storage to balance the supply with seasonal demands, and an appropriate burner. Such installations require authorisation from the local authority.

Oil storage regulations

These regulations apply to industrial and commercial businesses and institutional sites that store oil above ground in containers holding over 200 litres, including tanks, intermediate bulk containers, oil drums, and mobile bowsers. Garages now use a bund tank to store oil, this is a double skinned tank or a tank within a tank.

The manager of the new garage is looking at the different types of used oil storage container.

1 What is the name of the shape of each of these containers?

a)

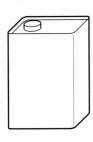

d)

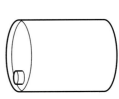

b)

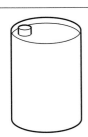

e)

c)

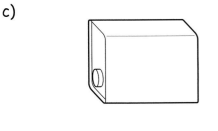

f)

2 Oil storage containers stand on bases. The names of the shapes of various different bases are given below. Draw each shape.

a) square

b) circle

c) rectangle

d) ellipse (commonly known as an oval)

e) octagon

f) equilateral triangle

The manager compares the volume of different tanks that are cuboids.

1   Calculate the volume in m³ of each tank shown below.

a) [   ]

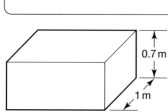

0.7 m
1 m
1.5 m

d) [   ]

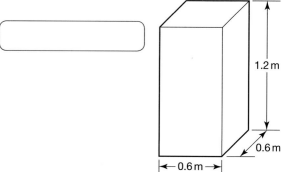

1.2 m
0.6 m
0.6 m

b) [   ]

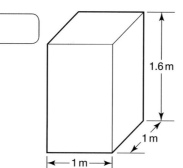

1.6 m
1 m
1 m

e) [   ]

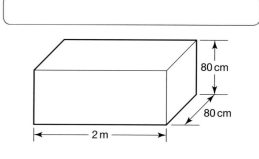

80 cm
80 cm
2 m

c) [   ]

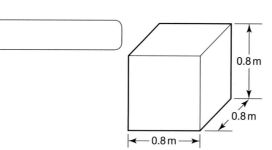

0.8 m
0.8 m
0.8 m

f) [   ]

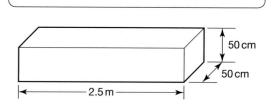

50 cm
50 cm
2.5 m

2   Calculate how many litres of used oil can be stored
    in each of the tanks in question 1.

Remember:
1 m³ = 1000 litres

a) [   ]   d) [   ]

b) [   ]   e) [   ]

c) [   ]   f) [   ]

3   The manager decides he wants a tank that will hold 1200 litres.

a) What will the volume of the tank be in m³?

[   ]

b) Suggest possible dimensions for a tank that would give that volume.

[   ]

L2

The manager compares the volume of different shapes of tank.

1   The formula for the volume of a cylinder is $\pi r^2 h$.

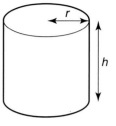

a) Use the formula to calculate the volume of tanks with the values for π, r and h given below. Give your answers correct to three decimal places.

i) $\pi = 3.14$; $r = 0.6$ m; $h = 1.2$ m

ii) $\pi = 3.14$; $r = 0.5$ m; $h = 1.5$ m

b) Calculate how many litres each of the above cylinders would hold.

i)

ii)

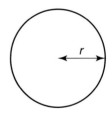

Remember:
$1\,m^3 = 1000$ litres

2   The formula for the volume of a sphere is $\frac{4}{3}\pi r^3$.

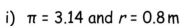

a) Use the formula to calculate the volume of tanks with the values for π and r below. Give your answers correct to three decimal places,

i) $\pi = 3.14$ and $r = 0.8$ m

ii) $\pi = 3.14$ and $r = 0.6$ m

b) Calculate how many litres each of the above would hold.

i)

ii)

3 The formula for a trapezium-shaped prism is $\dfrac{lh(a+b)}{2}$.

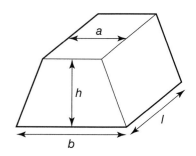

a) Use the formula to calculate the volume of tanks with the values for *l*, *h*, *a* and *b* given below. Give your answers correct to three decimal places.

   i) *l* = 1.2 m, *h* = 0.8 m, *a* = 0.6 m and *b* = 0.8 m

   ii) *l* = 1.4 m, *h* = 1.2 m, *a* = 0.8 m and *b* = 1 m

b) Calculate how many litres each of the above would hold.

   i)

   ii)

Perimeter, area and scale drawings

SOURCE Planning a staffroom 1

To meet health and safety regulations, the manager of a chain of motor vehicle workshops needs to add a room to existing buildings where staff can go to take a break. He has proposed the following options for the different sites.

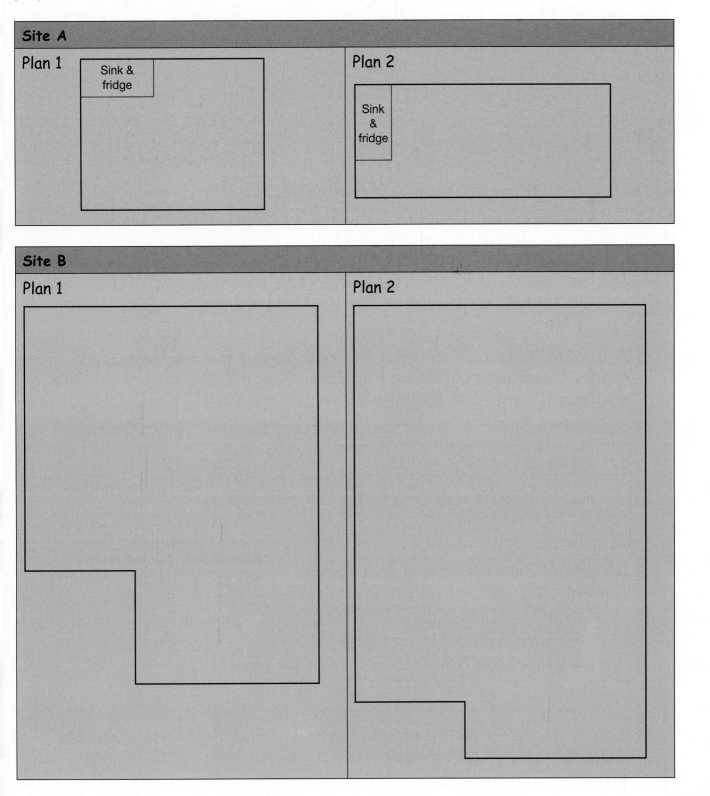

E3

Study the scale drawings for site A. The scale used is 1cm to 1m.

1 a) Measure the lengths for plan 1 and copy them onto the square paper below.

b) Measure the lengths for plan 2 and copy them onto the square paper below.

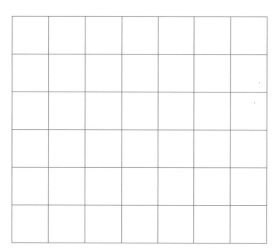

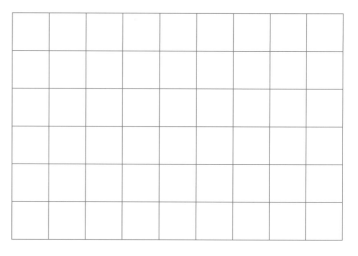

Use your drawings to answer the following questions.

2 a) Calculate the perimeter (distance round the edge) of the real building shown on plan 1.

Remember: 1cm on the drawing is 1m in the real building.

b) Calculate the perimeter of the real building shown on plan 2.

c) Some of the staff want as much wall space as possible to display posters and notices. If both plans are the same height and have the same size and number of windows and doors, which plan will have the most wall space?

3 a) Calculate the total floor area in square metres of plan 1 by counting the squares.

b) How much floor space is taken up by the sink and fridge?

c) Calculate the total floor area in square metres of plan 2.

Remember: Each square cm represents 1m^2 (square metre).

d) How much floor space is taken up by the sink and fridge?

e) Some of the staff think it is important to have as much floor space as possible. Which option should they choose?

Study the scale drawings for site B. The scale used is 1:50.

1 Sketch plans 1 and 2 below. Calculate the lengths of the actual walls using the scale given, and mark these on your sketches.

a) Plan 1

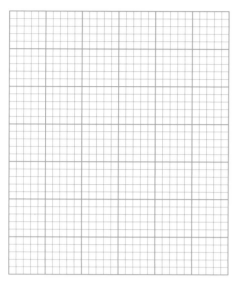

b) Plan 2

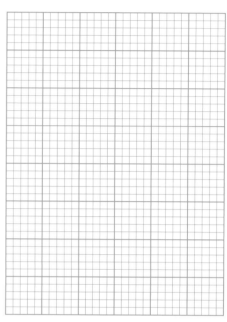

2 a) Calculate the perimeters of the actual buildings shown on:

(i) Plan 1

(ii) Plan 2

b) Some of the staff want as much wall space as possible to display posters and notices. If both plans are the same height and have the same size and number of windows and doors, which plan will have the most wall space?

3 a) Calculate the total floor area in square metres for:

(i) Plan 1

(ii) Plan 2

b) Some of the staff think it is important to have as much floor space as possible. Which option should they choose?

L2

Study the scale drawings for site B. The scale used is 1:40.

1   Sketch plans 1 and 2 below. Calculate the lengths of the actual walls using the scale given, and mark these on your sketches.

a) Plan 1

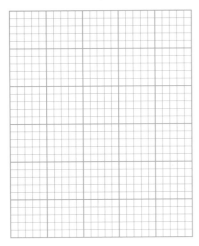

b) Plan 2

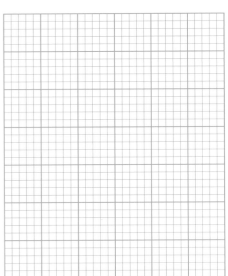

2   a) Calculate the perimeters of the actual buildings shown on:

(i) Plan 1

(ii) Plan 2

b) Some of the staff want as much wall space as possible to display posters and notices. If both plans are the same height and have the same size and number of windows and doors, which plan will have the most wall space?

3   a) Calculate the total floor area in square metres for:

(i) Plan 1

(ii) Plan 2

b) Some of the staff think it is important to have as much floor space as possible. Which option should they choose?

Perimeter, area and scale drawings

 **Planning a staffroom 2**

To meet health and safety regulations, the manager of a chain of motor vehicle workshops needs to add a room to existing buildings where staff can go to take a break. The staff are not happy with the options he has proposed and have submitted the following sketches.

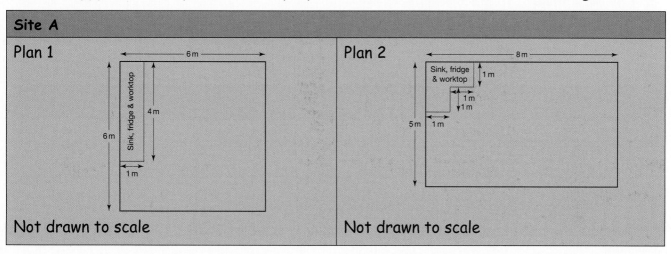

Site A

Plan 1

Not drawn to scale

Plan 2

Not drawn to scale

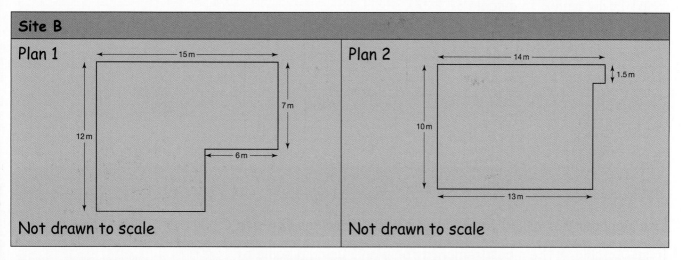

Site B

Plan 1

Not drawn to scale

Plan 2

Not drawn to scale

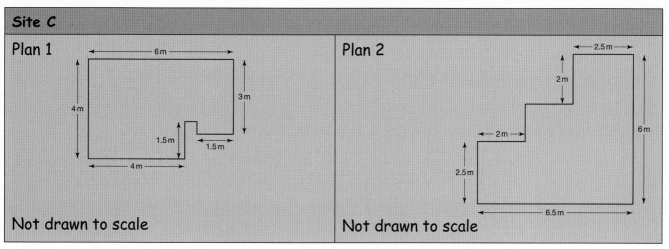

Site C

Plan 1

Not drawn to scale

Plan 2

Not drawn to scale

E3

The manager has asked for accurate scale drawings for site A.

1   Draw plan 1 for site A using a scale of 1 cm to 1 m.

2   Draw plan 2 for site A using a scale of 1 cm to 1 m.

L1

The manager has asked for accurate scale drawings for site B.

1   a)   Calculate the measurements for plan 1 using a scale of 1:50.

     b)   Draw plan 1 to a scale of 1:50.

2   a)   Calculate the measurements for plan 2 using a scale of 1:50.

     b)   Draw plan 2 to a scale of 1:50.

L2

The manager has asked for accurate scale drawings for site C.

1   a)   Calculate the measurements for plan 1 using a scale of 1:40.

     b)   Draw plan 1 to a scale of 1:40.

2   a)   Calculate the measurements for plan 2 using a scale of 1:40.

     b)   Draw plan 2 to a scale of 1:40.

Pages 85 and 86 are left blank for you to complete your drawings.

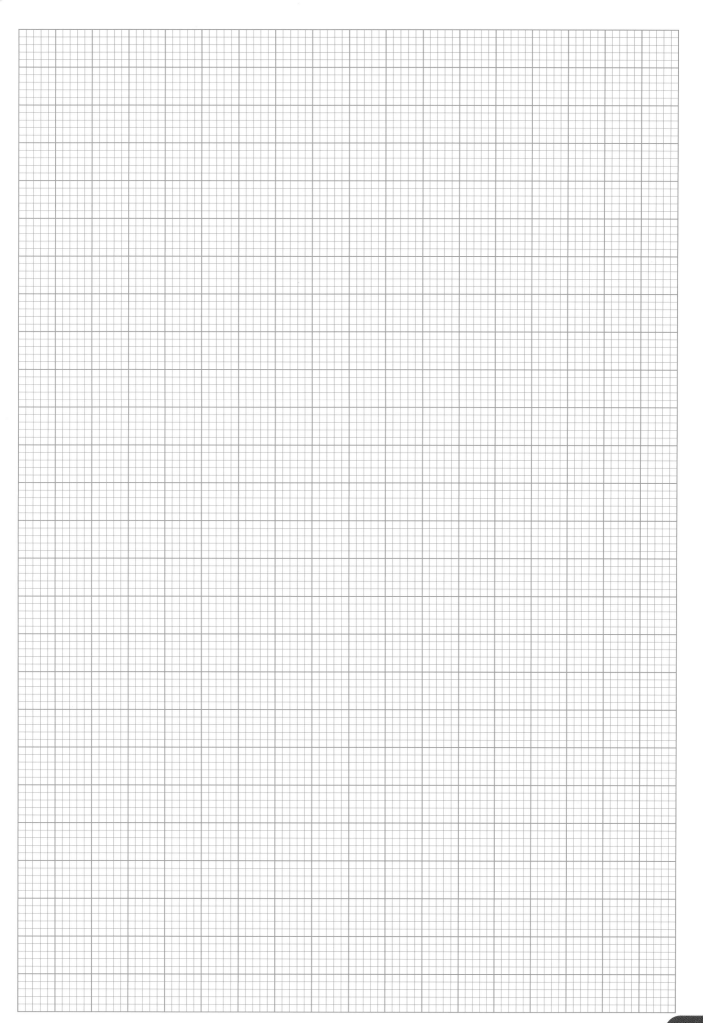

Measures, shape and space

Handling data

FOCUS ON Extracting data from tables, charts and graphs

Tables

In order to interpret the data in a table, you need to know what data it includes.

Number of reported accidents	Year				
Garage	2008	2009	2010	2011	2012
Brendon	5	4	6	8	4
Darwin	3	0	2	1	1
Fairview	2	4	3	3	2

Check the title and headings for columns.

Charts and graphs

Similarly, you also need to know what data is being presented in a graph or chart. For example, on this bar chart:

Check the title.

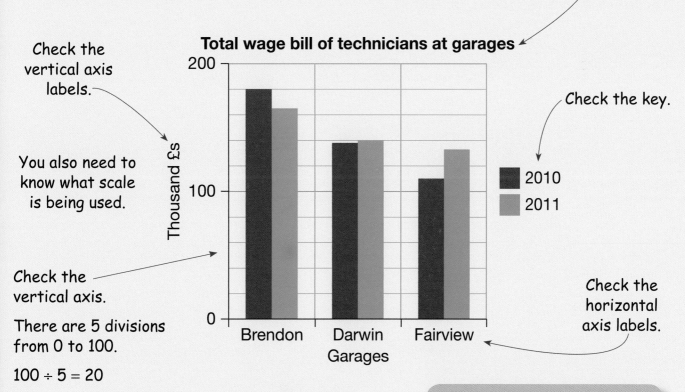

Check the vertical axis labels.

You also need to know what scale is being used.

Check the vertical axis.

There are 5 divisions from 0 to 100.

$100 \div 5 = 20$

So each division is worth 20 units, i.e. £20 000.

Check the key.

Check the horizontal axis labels.

Note: units are in thousands.

Here's another example of a graph:

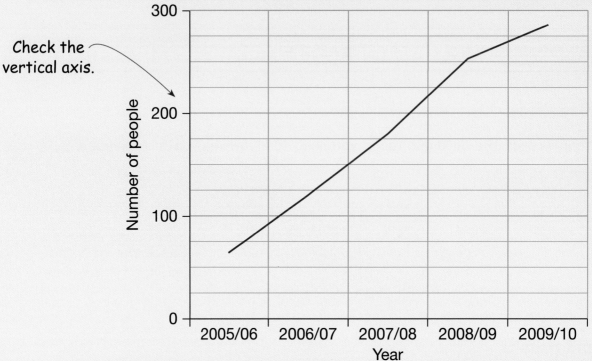

Number of people receiving 'drive from wheelchair vehicles'

Check the vertical axis.

There are 4 divisions from 0 to 100.

$100 \div 4 = 25$

So each small division represents 25 units, i.e. 25 people.

FOCUS ON Presenting data on charts and graphs

Choosing the right chart or graph

It is important to choose the correct method to display your data. Different charts and graphs are more appropriate for some types of data but not for others.

Bar graph Can be used to display discrete (separate) data or to compare data. For example: • the number of cars for sale in different garages • the number of new or previously-owned cars for sale.	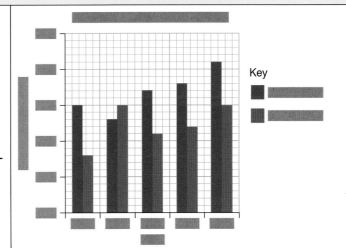
Line graph Can be used to display continuous data or trends. For example: • the number of cars sold • the number of miles travelled.	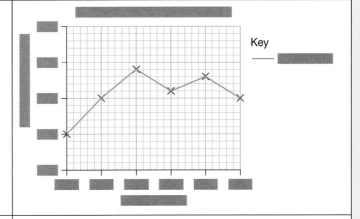
Pie chart Can be used to display proportion. For example: • the proportions of differently fuelled vehicles within the whole market/area • a breakdown of costs for a vehicle repair job.	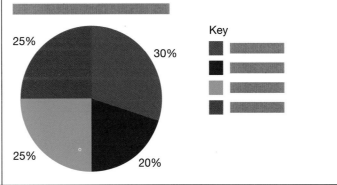
Scattergraph/scattergram Can be used to display correlation (the relationship between two variables). For example: • travel time vs. distance.	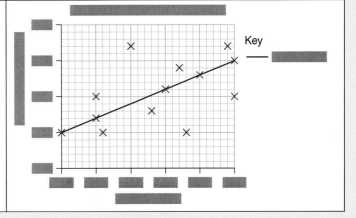

Drawing charts and graphs

Layout

Before you start to draw a graph or bar chart, decide on the largest number you need on the vertical axis. Then decide how many bars or points are needed along the horizontal axis.

Year	1	2	3	4	5	6
Amount (£)	75	118	92	75	60	48

The largest number is 118 so the vertical scale should reach 120.

Count up the large squares and choose a convenient scale, for example 1 large square = £10 or £20. It is usually easiest to count up in multiples of 5 or 10 as each large square has 5 or 10 small divisions on standard graph paper.

Six bars are needed for a bar chart with spaces between the bars. The bars should be the same width as each other. The spaces should be the same width as each other, but can be narrower than the bars.

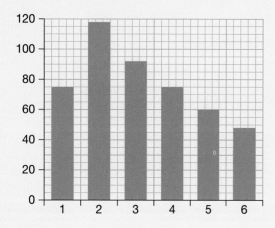

Labelling

All charts and graphs need a title.

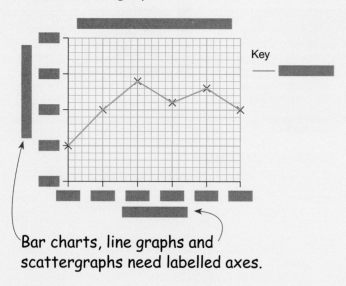

Bar charts, line graphs and scattergraphs need labelled axes.

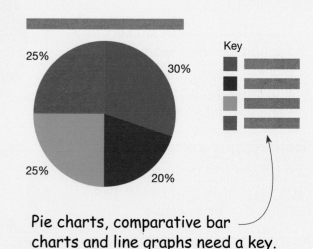

Pie charts, comparative bar charts and line graphs need a key.

FOCUS ON **Averages**

An average is a representative value of a set of data. The choice of mean, median or mode depends on the nature of the data and what the average is to be used for.

Mean average

The mean is calculated by adding all the values and dividing by the number of values. For example, in a group of people, the ages are:

  17   18   25   17   17   57   65   19   17   18   16

To calculate the mean, add the numbers together = 286

Then divide by the number in the group 286 ÷ 11 = 26

Therefore the mean average age is 26.

Note that the mean may be distorted by extreme values.

Mode

The mode is the most common value.

Using the data above, 17 is the mode as it occurs 4 times (18 occurs twice and the rest only once).

Note that there may be more than one mode or no mode at all.

Median

Put the numbers in order and find the middle number.

Using the data above, put the numbers in order and find the middle number.

  median   16   17   17   17   17   18   18   19   25   57   65

If there is an even number of values, find the midpoint between the two values in the middle. (You can do this by adding them together and dividing by 2.)

Range

The range indicates the spread of the data from the smallest value to the largest value. To calculate the range, subtract the smallest value from the largest.

Using the data above, 65 – 16 = 49.

Note that the smaller the range is, the more consistent the values are.

Extracting data from tables, charts and graphs

 **Working days lost through sickness**

In 2010/11 around 26.4 million working days were lost in total, 22.1 million due to work-related illness and 4.4 million due to workplace injuries.

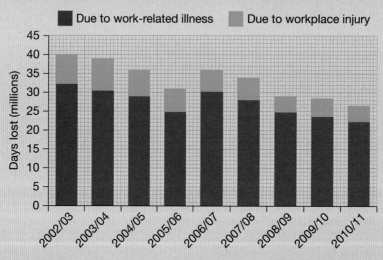

Working days lost due to work-related incidents

■ Due to work-related illness ■ Due to workplace injury

Self-reported illness caused or made worse by work

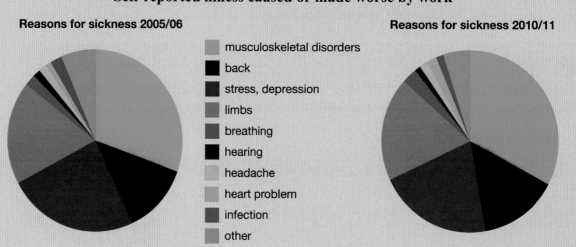

Reasons for sickness 2005/06

Reasons for sickness 2010/11

- musculoskeletal disorders
- back
- stress, depression
- limbs
- breathing
- hearing
- headache
- heart problem
- infection
- other

E3

Study the bar chart showing working days lost due to work-related incidents.

1   How many days are represented by each labelled division on the vertical axis?

2   Estimate the total number of working days lost and complete the following table.

Year	Total number of working days lost (in millions)	Year	Total number of working days lost (in millions)
2002/03		2007/08	
2003/04		2008/09	
2004/05		2009/10	
2005/06		2010/11	
2006/07			

3   In which year were the most working days lost through sickness?

4   In which year were the fewest working days lost through sickness?

5   Sara says the number of working days lost through sickness has dropped each year since 2002. Is she right? Explain.

6   Estimate the number of working days that will be lost due to sickness in 2015.

7   Do you think the records collected about reasons for sickness are always accurate? Explain.

L1

Study the bar chart showing working days lost due to work-related incidents.

1   Estimate the number of working days lost and complete the following table.

Year	Number of working days lost due to work-related illness (in millions)	Number of working days lost due to workplace injury (in millions)
2002/03		
2003/04		
2004/05		
2005/06		
2006/07		
2007/08		
2008/09		
2009/10		
2010/11		

2   Which of these statements are true and which are false, according to the data?

a) Between 2002 and 2011 days lost to workplace
   injuries reduced each year.   True ☐   False ☐

b) Days lost to workplace injuries in 2010/11 were
   about half the number they were in 2002/03.   True ☐   False ☐

c) Days lost to workplace injuries in 2010/11 were
   fewer than the number they were in 2009/10.   True ☐   False ☐

Study the pie charts showing self-reported illness caused or made worse by work.

3   List the reasons for sickness in order for 2005/06, starting with the most frequent
    reason given.

a) [　　　　　　　　]   f) [　　　　　　　　]

b) [　　　　　　　　]   g) [　　　　　　　　]

c) [　　　　　　　　]   h) [　　　　　　　　]

d) [　　　　　　　　]   i) [　　　　　　　　]

e) [　　　　　　　　]   j) [　　　　　　　　]

L2

Study the pie charts showing self-reported illness caused or made worse by work.

1   Which of these statements are true and which are false, according to the data?

   a) Half of the days lost through sickness in 2010/11 were due to back problems, musculoskeletal problems and reasons other than those listed.   True ☐   False ☐

   b) In 2005/06 about $\frac{1}{3}$ of the days lost through sickness were due to musculoskeletal problems.   True ☐   False ☐

   c) $\frac{1}{4}$ of the days lost through sickness in 2010/11 were due to problems with limbs.   True ☐   False ☐

   d) More people had days off sick with heart problems in 2010/11 than in 2005/06.   True ☐   False ☐

   e) In 2010/11 about $\frac{1}{4}$ of the days lost were due to stress and depression.   True ☐   False ☐

   f) More days were lost through stress and depression in 2010/11 than in 2005/06.   True ☐   False ☐

   g) Fewer people had days off sick with breathing problems in 2005/06 than in 2010/11.   True ☐   False ☐

   h) More than half of the days lost through sickness are caused by musculoskeletal disorders and problems with limbs and backs.   True ☐   False ☐

2   In 2010/11 about 1652000 days lost through sickness were reported to be caused or made worse by work. Approximately 31000 days were lost to problems with breathing. Use the chart to estimate the number of days lost for each reason below.

   a) Stress and depression

   b) Musculoskeletal disorders

   c) Headaches

   d) Infections

   e) Back problems

3   Write a newspaper headline based on your answer to question 2(a).

Extracting data from tables, charts and graphs

SOURCE Carbon emissions targets

The United Nations Kyoto Protocol set a target to reduce greenhouse gas emissions by 12.5% between 1990 and 2012. However, the UK government aimed for greater reductions: 22% by 2012, 28% by 2017, 34% by 2022 and 60% by 2050 (each reduction based on 1990 levels).

Sources of carbon emissions in the UK, 1990–2011 (million tonnes)									
Source	1990	1995	2000	2005	2007	2008	2009	2010	2011
Energy supplies	242	211	203	218	219	213	190	196	184
Transport	119	120	125	129	131	126	121	121	119
Business	111	104	104	94	89	87	76	76	70
Residential	79	81	87	84	78	80	75	87	67
Other	39	36	31	27	24	22	16	17	16

Domestic transport contribution to UK greenhouse gas emissions in 2009

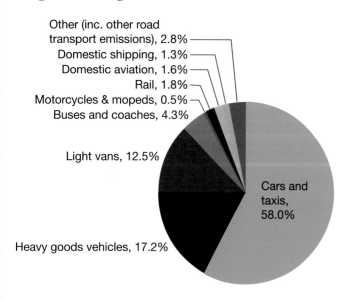

Other (inc. other road transport emissions), 2.8%
Domestic shipping, 1.3%
Domestic aviation, 1.6%
Rail, 1.8%
Motorcycles & mopeds, 0.5%
Buses and coaches, 4.3%
Light vans, 12.5%
Cars and taxis, 58.0%
Heavy goods vehicles, 17.2%

E3

Study the table showing sources of carbon emissions.

1 a) How many million tonnes of emissions were produced by transport in 1990?

b) In which other year did transport produce the same amount as in 1990?

c) In which year did transport produce the most emissions?

2 a) In which year did energy supplies produce the most emissions?

b) How much was produced?

c) In which year did energy supplies produce the least emissions?

d) How much was produced?

3 Find the total emissions in million tonnes produced for each of the years below.

a) 1990

b) 2000

c) 2010

d) 2011

4 Match the parts of the sentences about carbon emissions between 1990 and 2011.

a) Carbon emissions from transport have gone…	… up.
b) Other carbon emissions have gone…	… up or stayed the same.
c) Residential carbon emissions have gone…	… up and down.
d) Business carbon emissions have gone…	… down or stayed the same.
e) Carbon emissions from energy supplies have gone…	… down.

L1

Study the table showing sources of carbon emissions.

1 Find the difference between the most and least emissions produced for each source.

a) Energy supplies

b) Transport

c) Business

d) Residential

e) Other

Study the pie chart showing the domestic transport contribution to UK greenhouse gas emissions.

2 Which of these statements are true and which are false, according to the data?

a) Cars and taxis accounted for over $\frac{1}{2}$ of the emissions. True ☐   False ☐

b) Buses and coaches produced more than double
   the emissions from rail.   True ☐   False ☐

c) Light vans, motorcycles and mopeds produced
   the same emissions as heavy goods vehicles. True ☐   False ☐

d) Light vans accounted for $\frac{1}{8}$ of emissions.   True ☐   False ☐

e) Rail was the third-smallest contributor to emissions. True ☐   False ☐

f) Heavy goods vehicles emitted under $\frac{1}{3}$ of the
   emissions of cars and taxis.   True ☐   False ☐

3 Car and taxi emissions were roughly $4\frac{1}{2}$ times those produced by light vans. This could mean that there are two light vans for every nine cars or taxis.

Do you think there are two light vans for every nine cars or taxis? If not, what does this say about emissions from light vans?

L2

Study the table showing sources of carbon emissions.

1   In which year did transport account for:

a) about $\frac{1}{5}$ of the total emissions?

b) about $\frac{1}{4}$ of the total emissions?

c) more than $\frac{1}{4}$ of the total emissions?

2   a) How many tonnes did the Kyoto target want the UK to reduce its emissions by between 1990 and 2012?

b) When was this target achieved?

3   Calculate the total emission targets set by the UK government for:

a) 2012

b) 2017

c) 2022

d) 2050

4   Draw line graphs on the grid on the right to show UK emissions from 1990 to 2011, UK targets between 1990 and 2050 and the Kyoto reduction target for 2012.

5   Do you think the UK will meet the targets for 2017, 2022 and 2050? Explain.

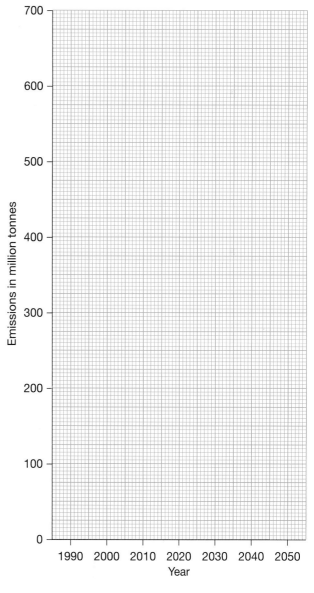

Carbon emissions in UK 1990–2011, Kyoto 2012 targets and UK targets 2012–2050

Emissions in million tonnes

Year

Key

—◆— UK emissions

—■— Kyoto target levels

—▲— UK target levels

Extracting data from tables, charts and graphs

 **Accidents on roads**

Each year in the UK, accidents involving motor vehicles cause thousands of injuries and claim too many lives. Every driver should be aware of driving conditions and their potential to contribute to accidents.

Vehicles involved in accidents with casualties						
	2005	2006	2007	2008	2009	2010
Pedal cycles	12039	16611	16607	16797	17599	17811
Motorcycles	25870	24323	24381	22427	21590	19534
Cars	281810	267991	255891	236923	227244	212685
Bus/coach	9988	9133	8559	8375	7831	7462
Light goods vehicles	16078	15593	14620	13621	13214	12866
Heavy goods vehicles	12120	11336	10688	9040	7487	7615

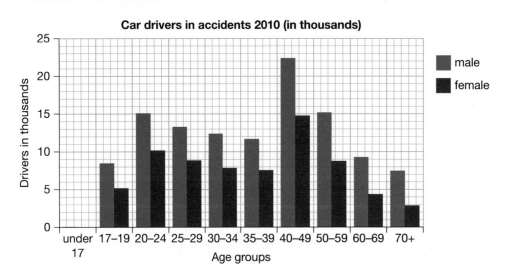

Car drivers in accidents 2010 (in thousands)

Driving conditions when accidents took place

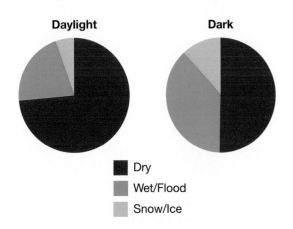

E3

Study the bar chart showing car drivers in accidents.

1 What is the value of each division on the vertical axis?

2 a) Which colour on the chart represents male drivers?

   b) Which colour on the chart represents female drivers?

3 Which age group, for each gender, has the most accidents?

a) Male drivers   b) Female drivers

4 Which drivers had fewer accidents in each age group – male or female?

5 Estimate the number of accidents for each set of drivers below.

a) Male 20–24   e) Female 20–24

b) Male 25–29   f) Female 25–29

c) Male 30–34   g) Female 30–34

d) Male 35–39   h) Female 35–39

6 Use your answers to question 5 to estimate the number of accidents for each of these groups.

a) Male drivers 20–29   c) Female drivers 20–29

b) Male drivers 30–39   d) Female drivers 30–39

7 Under 17s have very few accidents. Does this mean they are the best drivers? Explain.

8 Car insurance is higher for younger drivers. Do you think this is fair? Explain.

L1

Study the table showing vehicles involved in accidents with casualties.

1 Which of these options are true and which are false, according to the data?

Between 2005 and 2010 accidents with casualties reduced each year for:

a) pedal cycles   True ☐   False ☐

b) motorcycles   True ☐   False ☐

c) cars   True ☐   False ☐

d) light goods vehicles   True ☐   False ☐

2 Altogether how many accidents involved casualties in 2005?

3 How many fewer accidents were there in 2010?

Study the bar chart showing car drivers in accidents.

4 Estimate the difference in accident numbers between male and female drivers:

a) aged 17–19   c)   aged 30–39

b) aged 20–29   d)   aged 40–49

5 Jasmin says women are better drivers than men. Is she right? Explain.

Study the pie charts.

6 Estimate the percentage of accidents in daylight that can be attributed to:

a) wet or flooded conditions

b) snow or ice

7 Estimate the percentage of accidents in the dark that can be attributed to:

a) wet or flooded conditions

b) snow or ice

8 Estimate the percentage of accidents that happen in dry conditions:

a) in daylight

b) in darkness

L2

1   For each type of vehicle, find the percentage increase/decrease in accidents with casualties between 2005 and 2010.

a) Pedal cycles [   ]   d) Buses/coaches [   ]

b) Motorcycles [   ]   e) Light goods vehicles [   ]

c) Cars [   ]   f) Heavy goods vehicles [   ]

2   Estimate the fraction of accidents female drivers were involved in compared to men, in these age groups.

a) Aged 20–24 [   ]   c) Aged 60–69 [   ]

b) Aged 25–29 [   ]   d) Over 70 [   ]

3   Raman says the chart showing car drivers in accidents is misleading. Why is this?

4   Find the average number of accidents for each year of age within the age groups for male drivers between 17 and 49.

5   If all accidents in 2010 had happened in daylight, how many could have been attributed to:

a) wet or flooded conditions? [   ]

b) snow or ice? [   ]

6   If all accidents in 2010 had happened in darkness, how many could have been attributed to:

a) wet or flooded conditions? [   ]

b) snow or ice? [   ]

7   Write recommendations for learner drivers to go with the pie charts.

Extracting data from tables, charts and graphs

SOURCE Power and torque

The power of an engine is the ability to give speed to a vehicle over a period of time.

The torque of an engine is the ability to provide pulling power. This comes from the rotating crankshaft. The piston is pushed into the cylinder rod, forcing the crankshaft to rotate.

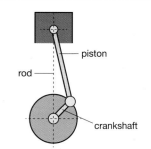

Piston and crankshaft

Piston strokes

Four cylinder in-line engine

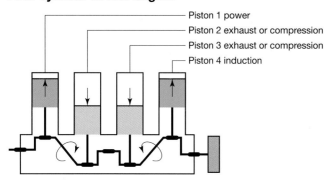

Piston 1 power
Piston 2 exhaust or compression
Piston 3 exhaust or compression
Piston 4 induction

Piston strokes	
If the crankshaft makes two full turns (rotations), there are four strokes, one at each half turn (180°).	
Stroke 1	Power
Stroke 2	Exhaust
Stroke 3	Induction
Stroke 4	Compression

Pistons move in pairs.

Here pistons 1 and 4 make power and compression strokes while pistons 2 and 3 make exhaust and compression strokes.

Firing order

One possible firing order starting with piston 1 is 1, 3, 4, 2.

Torque

Torque varies with engine design. The movement of air and fuel depends on the valves.

Many petrol engines have fixed valve timings where maximum torque is at medium engine speed (about 3500 rpm). Then torque reduces. Engine speed can still increase.

Modern engines have variable valve timings, giving a more consistent high torque.

Six cylinder in-line engine

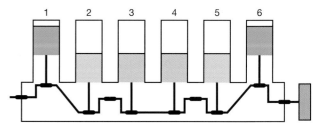

Torque curve 1

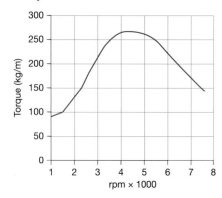

Torque curve 2

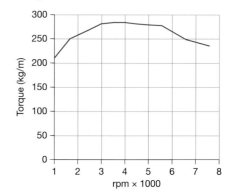

E3

1 Engines are designed to match the torque and power required for the use of a vehicle.

Put the following vehicles in the correct places in the table below.

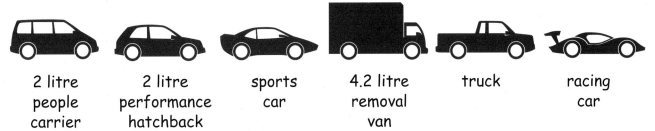

| 2 litre people carrier | 2 litre performance hatchback | sports car | 4.2 litre removal van | truck | racing car |

Good torque. Able to carry heavy loads. Generally a lower engine and road speed	Good power. Can reach high engine speeds

2 The highest torque is made when the rod is at right-angles to the crankshaft.

Circle the positions where the torque transfer is greatest.

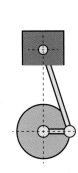 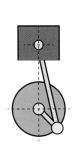 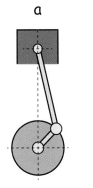 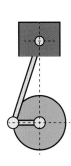

a   b   c   d

3 One firing order for the four-cylinder in-line engine is 1, 2, 4, 3.

a) If piston 1 starts with a power stroke, what are the next three strokes it makes?

b) What is the other possible firing order that starts with piston 1?

L1

1 The pistons on a six-cylinder in-line engine rotate in the order shown in the diagram. A possible firing order would be 1, 2, 3, 6, 5, 4.

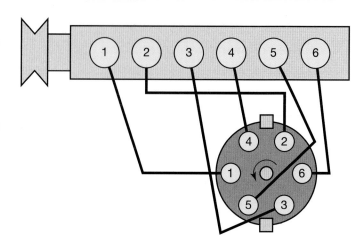

a) What are the other three possible firing orders starting with piston 1?

2 On the torque curve charts, what is shown on:

a) the horizontal axis?

b) the vertical axis?

3 a) Which of the torque curve charts shows an engine with fixed valve timings?

b) Explain your reasoning.

c) Which of the torque curve charts shows an engine with variable valve timings?

d) Explain your reasoning.

4 Which engine reaches maximum torque first?

L2

Study this torque and power curve for a typical petrol engine with fixed valve timings and then answer the following questions.

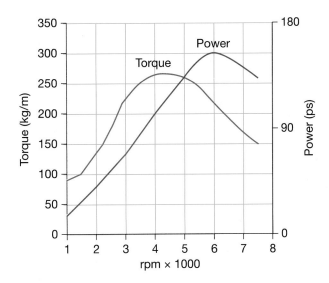

As speed rises, the inlet and exhaust valves have less time to release exhaust and gain fresh air and fuel, so torque output reduces. Power may remain, as there are more power strokes at the higher speed.

1 Estimate the rpm when valves start to lose enough time to emit exhaust.

2 Estimate the rpm when greatest power is reached.

3 Estimate the rpm when greatest torque is reached.

4 Estimate the torque values to complete the following table.

rpm	1000 rpm	2000 rpm	3000 rpm	4000 rpm	5000 rpm	6000 rpm	7000 rpm
Torque (kg/m)							

5 Estimate the power values (ps) to complete the following table.

rpm	1000 rpm	2000 rpm	3000 rpm	4000 rpm	5000 rpm	6000 rpm	7000 rpm
Power (ps)							

6 Delete the incorrect word in the following sentence.

With an engine with fixed valve timings, the torque produced is relatively low/high at low engine speeds.

Presenting data on charts and graphs

SOURCE Green cars

Concern for the environment is making many people consider alternatives to using fossil-fuelled cars. The advantages of electric cars include:

- no exhaust or emission tests
- no tune-ups
- no messy oil or antifreeze changes
- have 60–75% cheaper running costs
- less impact on the environment.

UK government encourages the purchase of electric cars with £5000 grants

According to a survey by Nielsen in 2010, $\frac{3}{4}$ of car owners in the UK either had or would have considered buying an electric car if the cost was comparable to the cost of oil- or diesel-powered cars. Since then, the number of people actually investing in alternatively fuelled cars has risen, as shown by the Department for Transport's figures in the table.

Number of electric, plug-in hybrid and hydrogen fuel-celled cars registered to owners in UK from January 2010 to March 2012								
Jan–Mar 2010	Apr–Jun 2010	Jul–Sep 2010	Oct–Dec 2010	Jan–Mar 2011	Apr–Jun 2011	Jul–Sep 2011	Oct–Dec 2011	Jan–Mar 2012
35	77	72	88	337	366	343	163	371

However, in 2010 J. D. Power and Associates reported that car owners were not aware of the costs of maintaining electric car batteries, recharging the batteries, the possible fuel savings or how far they could travel on one charge.

In northeast England 1000 charging stations have been installed as a trial and can be used free of charge until March 2013. After that, it is estimated that the cost of recharging a car will be £1.50.

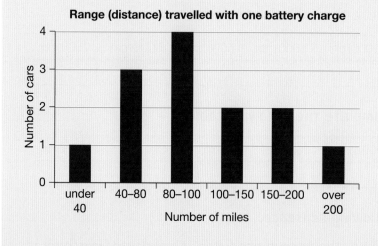

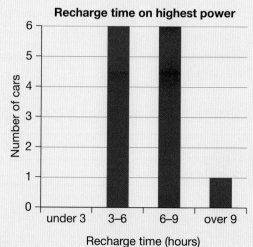

E3

1 Create a questionnaire that could be used to find out what people know about electric cars. Include questions on the advantages, disadvantages, travel distances, recharging, government grants, any trials and whether they would consider buying an electric car. Use the space below.

2 Ask about six to ten people to complete your questionnaire. Draw a chart to show the results.

L1

The bar charts show the range and battery recharge times for electric cars.

1 Design a data collection sheet that could be sent to car sales firms to collect data about the alternatively fuelled cars they have for sale.

2 Look on the internet for information about current electric and hybrid cars (for example www.gigaom.com/cleantech/battle-of-the-batteries-comparing-electric-car-range-charge-times).

Add this information to your data collection sheet above.

3 Draw a chart to represent some of the information you have found.

L2

1   Draw a line graph to show the data in the table on the number of electric, plug-in hybrid and hydrogen fuel-celled cars.

2   What sort of graph or chart would you use to represent the following data? Draw a rough sketch of what it might look like. Label the axes and/or key.

a) The number of people employed in manufacturing electric cars between 2000 and the current year

b) The proportion of cars sold in 2012 that were diesel, petrol or electric

c) A comparison of average costs between diesel, petrol and electric cars

Presenting data on charts and graphs

 **Drink-driving**

Drink-driving still causes many accidents on the roads.

Every driver should be aware of the potential risks of driving with too much alcohol in their blood – and of the legal consequences.

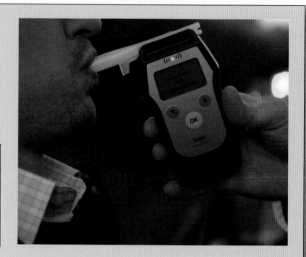

Recommended limits of alcohol before driving (units)		
	Immediately before	**The night before**
Men	4	10
Women	3	7

Prison sentences linked to drink-driving	
Driving with excess alcohol in the blood	6 months
In charge of a car with excess alcohol in the blood	3 months
Failing or refusing to supply a specimen when driving	6 months
Failing or refusing to supply a specimen when not driving	3 months
Causing death by careless driving with excess alcohol in the blood	14 years

Drink-driving offences (in thousands)							
	2000	**2001**	**2002**	**2003**	**2004**	**2005**	**2006**
Men	69	68	72	74	76	74	73
Women	8	9	9	10	10	10	11

Fatal accidents involving drink-driving									
	2000	**2001**	**2002**	**2003**	**2004**	**2005**	**2006**	**2007**	**2008**
Fatal accidents	450	430	480	500	520	470	490	370	380
Casualties killed	530	530	550	580	580	550	560	410	430

E3

1 a) Draw a bar chart to show the data in the table giving recommended limits of alcohol before driving.

b) Check that you have given your chart the following features.

Title ☐   Written in a scale ☐

Axis titles – horizontal and vertical ☐   Added a key for the coloured bars ☐

Labelled the bars ☐

2 Is it recommended that women drink less than men whenever they are driving?

3 Complete the pictogram to show the prison sentences linked with drink driving.

Offence	Months
Driving with excess alcohol in the blood	
In charge of a car with excess alcohol in the blood	
Failing or refusing to supply a specimen when driving	
Failing or refusing to supply a specimen when not driving	
Causing death by careless driving with excess alcohol in the blood	

Key:

6 months =

3 months =

L1

1 Draw a bar chart to show the data in the table giving numbers of drink-driving offences.

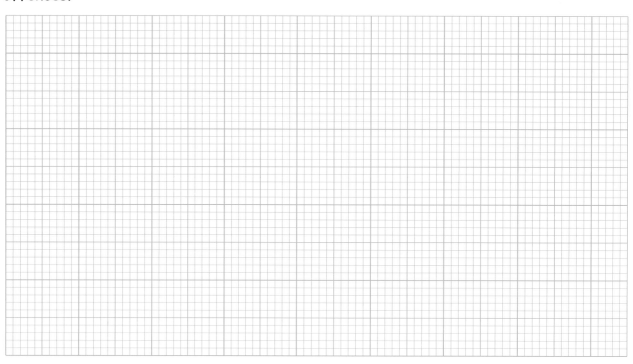

2 In approximately what proportion of the years from 2000 to 2006 were:

a) over 70000 drink-driving offences committed by men?

b) 10000 or more drink-driving offences committed by women?

3 It has been said that men commit over 90% of all drink-driving offences.

In which years was the proportion of men committing offences:

a) about 90%?

b) over 90%?

c) under 90%?

4 In which years were driving offences by women:

a) over $\frac{1}{8}$ of the number of offences by men?

b) less than $\frac{1}{8}$ of the number of offences by men?

c) $\frac{1}{8}$ of the number of offences by men?

L2

1 Draw a line graph to compare the fatal accidents and casualties killed between 2000 and 2008.

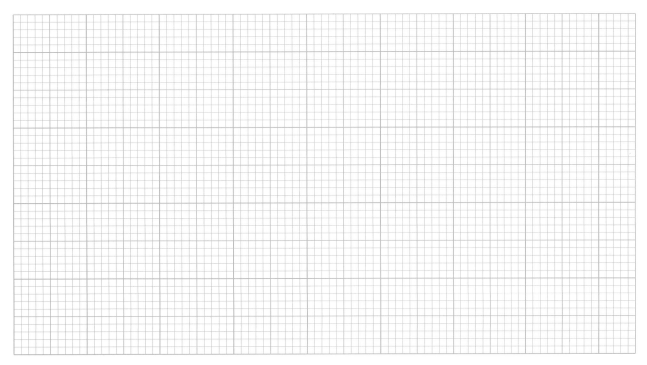

2 Comment on the change in the number of accidents and casualties after 2006.

3 Comment on the number of casualties compared to the number of accidents.

Interpreting data from charts and graphs

SOURCE **Car sales**

A car sales firm has 49 cars for sale, labelled with the age of the car and mileage.
Sam records the ages in years and mileage figures in thousands.

Age of cars (in years)

2	4	3	4	5	9	3
3	5	2	7	4	2	6.
2	5	8	7	5	2	1
3	1	5	4	4	3	3
4	7	6	1	2	3	2
3	5	2	8	4	3	3
4	3	8	6	3	2	4

Car mileage (in thousands)

31	54	33	49	95	98	35
48	51	21	62	47	18	42
5	62	79	87	81	42	13
41	16	66	68	42	31	39
54	89	71	7	25	40	27
37	63	28	87	48	26	33
47	24	97	75	41	21	32

E3

1 Record Sam's data on the cars' mileages in the tally chart below.

Count the tallies for each age and record the totals in the frequency column.

Mileage range of cars (in thousands)	Tally	Frequency
0–10		
11–20		
21–30		
31–40		
41–50		
51–60		
61–70		
71–80		
81–90		
91–100		
	Total:	

2 Find the total for the frequency column and add it to your chart. (This should equal the number of cars for sale.)

3 Draw a tally chart similar to the one above to record Sam's data on the cars' ages.

4 Find the total of the frequency column to check you have included all the cars. Add it to your chart.

5 What age of car is the most common?

6 What mileage range is the most common?

L1

1 Use Sam's data on the cars' mileages to draw a bar chart. Group the data into appropriate ranges of mileage and arrange them along the horizontal axis. Put the number of cars up the vertical axis.

2 Use Sam's data on the cars' ages to draw a bar chart.

3 How many cars are:

a) between 1 and 3 years old?

b) between 4 and 6 years old?

c) 7 or more years old?

L2

1 Write the frequency of each age of car and complete the third column.

Age of car (years)	Frequency	Age × frequency	Age of car (years)	Frequency	Age × frequency
1			6		
2			7		
3			8		
4			9		
5			Total:		

2 Use Sam's data to find the following statistics on the ages of the cars.

a) Mean

c) Mode

b) Median

d) Range

3 Write the frequency for each mileage range. Then, by using the mid-point for the range, complete the fourth column.

Mileage range of cars (in thousands)	Frequency	Mid-point of mileage range (in thousands)	Mid-point × frequency (in thousands)
0–10		5	
11–20		15.5	
21–30		25.5	
31–40		35.5	
41–50		45.5	
51–60		55.5	
61–70		65.5	
71–80		75.5	
81–90		85.5	
91–100		95.5	
Total:		Total:	

4 Use Sam's data to find the following statistics on the mileage ranges of the cars.

a) Mean

c) Mode

b) Median

d) Range

Interpreting data from charts and graphs

 **SOURCE** Petrol costs

Statistics show that car running costs depend on where you live. They also show that you can save money by shopping around.

Average unleaded petrol costs (pence per litre) for June 2010–June 2012			
Region	June 2010	June 2011	June 2012
Northern Ireland	118.8	137.4	135.3
Scotland	117.8	136.3	133.5
Wales	118.4	136.3	133.7
North	117.1	135.8	133.6
Northwest	116.9	135.6	133.5
Yorkshire & Humberside	116.8	135.4	133.2
West Midlands	117.7	136.0	133.6
East Midlands	117.6	135.7	133.7
East Anglia	118.6	136.4	133.9
Southeast	119.0	136.5	134.2
Southwest	118.3	136.2	134.1
London	119.3	136.1	134.0

Average petrol costs (pence per litre), 2006–2012				
	2006	2008	2010	2012
Garage: unleaded	95.9	118.2	118.1	133.8
Garage: super unleaded	101.5	125.1	125.4	141.6
Garage: diesel	98.1	131.6	120.5	139.3
Supermarket: unleaded	94.8	116.5	116.3	130.9
Supermarket: super unleaded	98.3	121.4	121.7	135.7
Supermarket: diesel	97.0	129.4	118.7	136.3

E3

Study the data on average unleaded petrol costs for June 2010–June 2012.

1   Which region had the most expensive unleaded petrol in:

   a) June 2012?

   b) June 2011?

   c) June 2010?

2   Which region had the cheapest unleaded petrol in:

   a) June 2012?

   b) June 2011?

   c) June 2010?

Study the data on average petrol costs for 2006–2012.

3   Round the figures for the garage petrol costs between 2006 and 2012 to the nearest penny. Complete the table.

Garage prices	2006	2008	2010	2012
Unleaded				
Super unleaded				
Diesel				

4   Which was the most expensive fuel in:

   a) 2006?

   b) 2008?

   c) 2010?

   d) 2012?

5   Use your rounded figures from question 3 to complete the comparative bar chart below. Label the axes and give the chart a title.

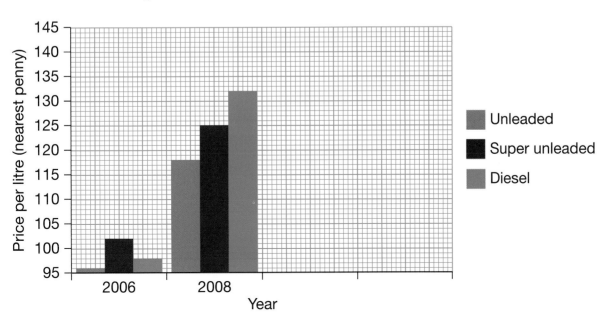

L1

Study the data on average petrol costs for 2006–2012.

1   Use the data to find the type of fuel in garages between 2006 and 2012 with:

   a) the largest price increase [   ]

   b) the smallest price increase [   ]

   c) Did the same fuels have the largest and smallest increases at supermarkets? Show your working.

2   Use the data to find the mean price and the price range for:

   a) garage petrol prices in 2006:

      (i) mean price [   ]

      (ii) price range [   ]

   b) supermarket petrol prices in 2006:

      (i) mean price [   ]

      (ii) price range [   ]

   c) garage petrol prices in 2012:

      (i) mean price [   ]

      (ii) price range [   ]

   d) supermarket petrol prices in 2012:

      (i) mean price [   ]

      (ii) price range [   ]

3   Would you recommend buying petrol from garages or supermarkets? Explain.

L2

1 Find the following prices for unleaded petrol:

a) mean price in June 2010

b) median price in June 2010

c) mode price in June 2010

d) mean price in June 2012

e) median price in June 2012

f) mode price in June 2012

2 Compare your mean figures for June with the average figures for unleaded petrol in the years 2010 and 2012. Do you think the table of prices by region included garages and supermarkets? Explain.

3 Which type of chart would be most effective for showing the trend in petrol prices between 2006 and 2012? Give your reasoning.

> comparative bar chart   line graph   pie chart

4 Which type of chart would be most effective for showing the petrol prices per region in 2012?

> bar chart   comparative bar chart   line graph

5 Which type of chart would be most effective for showing the changing petrol prices in Ireland, Scotland and Wales between 2010 and 2012?

> comparative line graph   comparative bar chart   line graph

Interpreting data from charts and graphs

Kristian's Mini needs a service. He compares prices to choose the various spare parts. He needs three litres of oil, a pack of spark plugs, an oil filter, an air filter, a pollen filter, new front and rear brake pads and new front and rear brake discs.

Engine oil

	4 litres	1 litre
Brand A	£51.99	£21.99
Brand B	£46.99	£15.99
Brand C	£39.99	£17.99
Brand D	£37.99	£15.99
Brand E	£42.99	£16.99

Spark plugs (per set)

Brand A	£7.64
Brand B	£10.74
Brand C	£21.68
Brand D	£29.00
Brand E	£31.00
Brand F	£22.38
Brand G	£10.40

FILTERS

	Oil filter		Air filter		Pollen filter
Brand A	£7.80	Brand A	£9.96	Brand A	£20.34
Brand B	£6.45	Brand B	£17.99	Brand B	£23.10
Brand C	£5.42	Brand C	£11.52	Brand C	£16.20
Brand D	£6.45	Brand D	£6.45		
Brand E	£8.92	Brand E	£15.52		
Brand F	£17.54				

BRAKE SPARES

	Brake pads			Brake discs	
	Front (per pair)	Rear (per pair)		Front (per pair)	Rear (per pair)
Brand A	£34.07	£25.56	Brand A	£61.81	£37.08
Brand B	£77.48	£50.15	Brand B	£54.04	£42.15
Brand C	£33.50	£27.75	Brand C	£16.74	£13.50
Brand D	£24.60	£19.80	Brand D	£25.80	£20.34
Brand E	£16.20	£15.00	Brand E	£76.99	£39.99
Brand F	£31.99	£27.99	Brand F	£47.99	£30.99

E3

1   The Mini needs three litres of oil.

   a) Which is the most expensive brand?

   b) Which is the cheapest brand and size to buy? Explain.

2   Which is the cheapest brand and price for these parts?

   a) spark plugs

   b) a new oil filter

   c) a new air filter

   d) a new pollen filter

   e) front brake pads

   f) rear brake pads

   g) front brake discs

   h) rear brake discs

3   What is the total cost of choosing the cheapest parts with the cheapest oil?

4   Which is the most expensive brand and price for these parts?

   a) spark plugs

   b) a new oil filter

   c) a new air filter

   d) a new pollen filter

   e) front brake pads

   f) rear brake pads

   g) front brake discs

   h) rear brake discs

5   What is the total cost of choosing the most expensive parts with the most expensive oil?

6   How much would Kristian save by buying the cheaper parts?

L1

1 Find the range in the prices for each of the following.

a) 4 litres of oil

b) 1 litre of oil

c) spark plugs

d) oil filter

e) air filter

f) pollen filter

g) front brake pads

h) rear brake pads

i) front brake discs

j) rear brake discs

2 Why do you think there might be such a large price range for some items?

3 Would you always buy the cheapest item? Explain.

4 Round the prices of all the brands of each of the following items to the nearest pound. Then find the mean price for each item.

a) oil filter

b) air filter

c) pollen filter

L2

Find the mean and median price of each of the following items.

a) spark plugs

    (i) mean

    (ii) median

b) front brake pads

    (i) mean

    (ii) median

c) rear brake pads

    (i) mean

    (ii) median

d) front brake discs

    (i) mean

    (ii) median

e) rear brake discs

    (i) mean

    (ii) median

2 Find the mean, median and modal price for the oil filters.

    a) mean

    b) median

    c) mode

3 If you were asked to give someone the average price for any of the above items, which average would you choose? Explain.

Acknowledgements

The author and the publisher would also like to thank the following for permission to reproduce material:

Text

p10 Copyright 2012 © topgear.co.uk; p18 © 2012 DriverSide Inc; p22 from www.imperialoil.ca; p39 Vauxhall Meriva Owner Manual, Vauxhall Edition 2007; pp43, 101, 106, 114 Department for Transport © Crown Copyright 2012. Reproduced under PSI licence 2009002012; p44 from www.roadtaxprices.co.uk; p44 © SMMT, 2012; pp60, 127 © The Automobile Association Limited 2012; p68 adapted from www.tyresave.co.uk © C.D. Clubbe; p72 © 2012 Kwik-Fit (GB) Limited; p76 from Environment Agency: Pollution Prevention Guidelines © Enviroment Agency 2012; p88 chart data from motability.co.uk; p95 Statistics showing working days lost through sickness from Health and Safety Executive © Crown Copyright 2012. Reproduced under PSI licence 2009002012; p101 Statistical Release from Department of Energy and Climate Change: *2011 UK Greenhouse Gas Emissions, Provisional Figures and 2010 UK Greenhouse Gas Emissions, Final Figures by Fuel Type and End User*, 29th March 2012 © Department of Energy and Climate Change; p118 © 2012 www.drinkdriving.org; p118 from www.80mg.org.

Images

Alamy: p10 (Iain Masterton), p18 (Drive Images), p22 (Jonathan Larsen/Diadem Images), p34 (Tetra Images), p42 (Corbis Flirt), p58 (Graham Oliver), p70 right (Christoph Weiser), p70 left (David Burton), p74 (Construction Photography), p102 (Peter Jordan_NE), p114 (67photo), p118 top (geophoto), p118 bottom (Mark Richardson), p127 (Sally Ann Baines); iStockphoto: p14 (struti), p26 (AlexKosev), p66 (svariophoto), p98 (ollo); Shutterstock: p35 (berkut); p92 (Monkey Business Images); Toyota (GB) PLC, with permission: p110; Volkswagen UK and Volkswagen AG: p10.

Every effort has been made to trace the copyright holders but if any have been inadvertently overlooked the publisher will be pleased to make the necessary arrangements at the first opportunity.